Improvisation
A PRACTICAL GUIDE

Improvisation
A PRACTICAL GUIDE

Jason Moran

THE CROWOOD PRESS

First published in 2021 by
The Crowood Press Ltd
Ramsbury, Marlborough
Wiltshire SN8 2HR

enquiries@crowood.com

www.crowood.com

British Library Cataloguing-in-Publication Data
A catalogue record for this book is available from the British Library.

ISBN 978 1 78500 931 0

Disclaimer
Every reasonable effort has been made to trace and credit copyright holders. In the event of an omission, please contact the publisher, who will be pleased to add a credit in any future edition.

Designed and typeset by Guy Croton Publishing Services, West Malling, Kent

Printed and bound in India by Parksons Graphics

CONTENTS

ACKNOWLEDGEMENTS

I would like to thank the Viola Spolin estate, specifically Aretha Sills and Carol Sills, for their support on the history of improvisation, and to Bloomsbury Publishing for their support with the same subject matter.

I must say a big thank you to all the great improvisers that have come and gone before us, and to the teachers and performers I have met over the years.

I'd like to thank my mother, Colette Moran, and my aunt, Vera Wegner, for their support and input on the human side of improvisation, and its benefits around mental health specifically, and to my partner, Alexis Moore, for keeping me motivated throughout.

Also, thank you to Jake Lyons for his friendship and mentorship over the years; indeed thanks go to all the *Livewired* comedy improvisation troupe (hereafter referred to simply as Livewired) and its community, past and present, as well as the London Improv Theatre.

Special thanks go to Jonathan for his diligence and research on the history of improvisation, and to Pali for her input in this text. (Both made appearances in the illustrations, along with Emma; other actors appearing are Tom, Katie and Paul from *Livewired*.) A final big thanks goes to Andrei for photographing the images.

Photo and illustrations: Andrei Avram.

Actors: Jonathan Reed, Pali Jhita, Emma Birkett, Tom Lovegrove, Katie Colley and Paul Whyman.

History of Improvisation: compiled by Jonathan Reed.

The Dark Side of Improv: written by Pali Jhita.

Improvisation and Mental Health Colette Moran BA and Vera Wegner MACBT, MIACP.

PREFACE

The one thing we all have in common is the unknown: what's going to happen next? As children we knew no different – we relied on the people around us to guide us through our early life, our parents, siblings, grandparents, cousins, teachers, friends, schools and community. Life was joyous, and everything we did we wanted to do right, we wanted to aspire and to learn. For some it was academic – to read, study, or be good at maths – for others it was sport, while yet others loved the manual work that occupied their parents, such as farming or working with machinery, tailoring or working as a seamstress, or cooking and baking. It didn't matter, there was something in all of us that drove that early passion and joy of learning something new. But at some point the unknown became scary and made us feel unstable, and as creatures of habit we built ourselves a routine to make our lives predictable and keep us feeling safe.

My acting journey started early in life, when as a child I went to a local speech and drama class: something about it made me feel at home. I wasn't a good footballer, nor was I particularly cool or popular, but in this class I felt as if I had found my place. This feeling never left me, and as I grew into adulthood I continued to enjoy and train in theatre and acting.

As an actor I loved the predictability, routine and ceremony of performing in a play: arriving at the theatre at the same time each evening, having a snack and a pre-show shower, then the application of make-up and costume, and lastly a light warm-up before going on stage. This routine made me feel safe, and it became part of the ceremony in preparing for the show – and if one item in this routine was left out it had a knock-on effect that rippled through the entire performance of the play on that occasion.

Improvisation to me then was a simple tool I would use if I forgot or miscued my lines, or if a fellow actor forgot their lines: then one of us would 'wing it' and improvise lines to get us back on track. It is also a common practice of many directors to use improvisation as a rehearsal mechanism while we work out our characters. I have used this technique myself with actors whom I have directed, and I still do.

In truth I never appreciated the full depth of this art form until I randomly walked into an improv class – and there it began. In that room on that day were a few other actors like me, looking to take a short course and thereby strengthen a skill long forgotten since drama school. There were also marketeers, advertising producers, dancers, stand-up comedians, people looking to improve their confidence and public-speaking skills, and some just looking to have fun.

All of us were uncertain, nervous and excited. We were already sharing the magic of improvisation before the class even started, and what happened with us over the next weeks, months and years I have seen happen hundreds of times since with the groups I have taught, coached and directed. A bond formed that none of us ever forgot.

To this day I am still in touch with most of those in that first improvisation class. I have carried on doing acting projects with some of these people, while others I have trained and worked with as we continued our improv journey and training.

Some of us have continued our careers as actors, comedians, teachers, while others have moved to direction, production, dance, music – and the people not involved in performance arts have continued to use their improvisation training in their worlds of advertising production or as corporate facilitators or trainers. When we reunite once a year or so we can still remember our first improvised scenes with each other, and the joy we shared all those years ago.

What tends to fascinate people most when watching improv, especially for the first time, is the idea that a structured story with rounded characters can be made up, right there on the spot and with no preparation. I can remember myself as a young teenager watching *Whose Line Is It Anyway?* in both the US and UK versions, doubting the authenticity of the show, wondering if the actors really were making it up, thinking they must have had a tip-off before the show, or been given a template to work from. This couldn't be real. Even my mother, who has spent a lot of time also treading the boards, had some degree of doubt.

How wrong I was! Once the skills of improvisation were explained and taught to me, and I began to apply them in improvised scene building, my view began to change. I even came to a point where I'd prefer to improvise completely instead of working from a script. And as you can imagine, this is a complete turnaround for someone whose initial training was traditional acting.

Now looking back at my doubts of how authentic improv is, I can't imagine ever having, or wanting to have, any kind of tip-off as to what I might be doing in a scene or game – and this will be the same for any active improviser you speak to. Not having the magic of the unknown would hold us back, as it is the spontaneity and discovery of improvising that drives the art form.

INTRODUCTION

People often say that life is one long improvised session. For some people it is natural: they can wake up in the morning and are happy to 'let the chips fall where they may', and take everything in their stride. This is not to say that these people don't follow a routine, as they would follow a routine as normal as the rest of us – they would be woken by an alarm, would exercise, shower, eat, commute, work, socialize, go home, eat, wind down and sleep: but their approach to all of these activities would be to meet each circumstance as it happened, and variation and a last-minute change of plans would not bother them. In other words, they have no problem with being spontaneous.

Others have a great capacity to think on their feet in social conversations or when presenting work in a more formal environment. They appear to have a depth of information that is stored and accessible in their heads, and which can be conjured up when required. The truth of it is that they can hold the stage long enough to give themselves a chance to find the information they need, or to use techniques to hold the conversation and be comfortable outside their comfort zone. All these things require practice and an element of confidence, but they are skills that can be attained over time as people grow. Improvisation makes people braver with their decisions, and encourages curiosity and an open mind-set.

It goes without saying that improvisation has many transferable skills that people can take into their personal and professional lives. It is also a useful training for people who may have no intention of performing in public, but which when applied can reap great benefits. It also comes into use when dealing with anything creative.

What this means to me is that every idea grows from a spark, so it needs to be heard – to be understood and built on. And if what is added is not working for the artist, it has at least removed a certain avenue of investigation, and the artist can move on in another direction.

Music also owes a great deal to improvisation, as any musicians who are reading this will acknowledge, when they consider the number of times they have sat with their instruments and played around with a few notes or chords, maybe with some lyric or even just a feeling, and from these beginnings have organically cultivated a song.

It is also not unusual for a group of musicians within a band to use improvisation when working with each other, sometimes in an informal way when playing around for fun or in order to come up with ideas, but also in the performance itself, making small adjustments that may or may not evolve and become a part of the official act.

Improvising in the moment is best recognized in sport, for example where a great footballer such as Ronaldo might improvise with a flick of the shoulder in a movement so fast that if they were to think about it, the moment and the opportunity would be gone. Having the skill and confidence to react instantly brings us opportunities, knowing and believing that in that moment it is the right thing to do. My favourite sporting improvised moment of all is Maradona in the 1986 World Cup quarter-final game against England, where he improvised and scored the most talked-about goal ever scored in a World Cup competition. Controversial? Absolutely! Premeditated? Personally, I don't think so. Genius? Yes, a great example of improv, showing risk and reward.

As I started to put this book together and looked at my own journey into improvisation, my feeling always led me back to what I would have read when I was starting out. What practical things would help me become a better improviser? Does just theory work? Would practical steps, with simple tips and tricks, be enough? Or do you need to find the right balance?

So it is clear that improvisation can be understood and used in different ways, depending on the need.

As you continue your journey you should see that all of these are valid. And taking these into your life as a performer and an individual is more important, as it makes your improvisation more believable. Over the course of my teaching I have seen the most unlikely people become amazing improv performers. They have begun in simple ways, such as having that belief in themselves to stand there with nothing and just trusting their spontaneity; then applying the practical steps that you learn to get stories and scenes up and running; understanding some theory enough to make you creative in your own space by using the tools and the processes that exist as an unwritten agreement with your co-improvisers; and the most important rule of all: having fun.

Remember the joy we had as children when all the world was joyous, and failure did not exist. We did so many amazing things as we grew up, things that we would struggle to do now: learning to walk, speak and understand an entire language, communicating with people around us, reading and writing, riding a bike. We have been improvising since the day we arrived, and we continue to do so.

HISTORY

Open most improvisation books, or research it on the internet, and you will probably find that most consider Commedia Dell'Arte to be the closest great-grandparent to improvisation as we know it today. Originating in the 1500s, it was made up of several stock characters that would recur in performances, the scenarios and storyline changing each time. The popularity of this roaming improv troupe was evident throughout Europe for 200 years, and due to the variety of dialects across Italy and of languages across southern Europe, the performance relied on strong gestures – sometimes obscene – a high level of physicality, such as jumping around the stage, and slapstick comedy. As chaotic as this may have seemed, the performers were in fact working together as an ensemble, and supported each other's ideas as well as the reaction of the audience – in much the same way as improvisation actors today.

Improvisation as a tool for the theatre came to two people at the same time, on opposite sides of the Atlantic: Viola Spolin in the USA, who developed her programme of theatre games in the late 1920s and 1930s, and Keith Johnstone in the UK, who developed his tools for rehearsal in the 1950s. The story of how these two pioneers developed and refined the use of games as a tool for rehearsal and theatre is the driving factor behind the development of modern improvisation on both sides of the Atlantic.

In the late 1920s and 1930s Viola Spolin began to experiment with using improvisational games as a rehearsal tool, having been inspired by a former teacher who placed an emphasis on the use of play. She devised a series of theatre games to create spontaneity in a performance, and practised and refined these in Chicago in various groups. Her son, Paul Sills, used these games in a newly formed theatre group – The Compass Players – to create a new kind of show.

What started as a means of creating narrative pieces eventually evolved into a variety show based on shorter scenes and games. The Compass Players gave a start to what became the well-known double acts of Elaine May and Mike Nichols, and Jerry Stiller and Anne Meara. But it also had amongst its early alumni Del Close, who was to become instrumental in the development of improvisation in the USA.

In 1959, Paul Sills, along with Bernie Sahlins and Howard Alk, set up The Second City, which developed the improvisational techniques of The Compass Players into full revues. Though Second City used improvisation to create scripted material and revues, it was Del Close who developed improvisation into a performance style. In 1981 he set up Improv Olympic (later known as IO) with Charna Halpern to pursue this style, which became the home of their signature piece the 'Harold'.

The 'Harold' was developed in 1967 as a form that would present several of the tools available to improvisers in one form – the monologue, the scene and the group game – and it is still one of the most popular long forms practised today. Many of the skills of good long-form improvisation (see below) are contained within it, and it is often learned first as a basis for learning other forms.

From this starting point came a huge variety of forms that provided new and innovative ways to structure long-form improvisation.

The US improv circuit gave the first break to a large proportion of the US comic talent. Bill Murray, Mike Myers, John Belushi, Amy Poehler and Tina Fey are just some of the many comedians who started their careers on a US improv theatre stage.

Back in the UK, Keith Johnstone was developing his own theatre games to help him direct at the Royal Court Theatre. Having no formal drama training himself, he changed from using the most modern techniques and instead invented his own games to bring out the relationships between the cast members. Keith started demonstrating his techniques, but they were so successful and enjoyable to watch that the cast started performing, rather than demonstrating. The newly formed improvisational theatre was called 'Theatre Machine', and was commissioned by the British Council to tour Europe. Later moving to Canada, Keith Johnstone established the Loose Moose Theatre and Theatre Sports, a licensed format of competitive improv games.

Improv returned to the UK again in the 1980s after – as the story goes – Mike Myers taught improv to the Comedy Store Players, established in 1985. They were a big hit, and several members joined the cast of *Whose Line Is It Anyway?*, a short-form improv show that aired on UK television from 1988 to 1999, and then later on US television from 1998. Now, the UK improv scene is thriving, with several theatres and styles on show.

Traditional theatre still uses improvisation as a tool, allowing actors to explore their characters in more depth and in film making. Many directors encourage actors to surprise their co-actors, in order to instil real reactions. Improvisation is used in both drama and comedy. One of the most famous improvised scenes is Joe Pesci's improvised 'Funny how' scene in Martin Scorsese's *Goodfellas*. Although this scene was subsequently written and heavily rehearsed before being shot, the idea came from a real experience, and when shared with the director, it was suggested that initially it should be improvised.

Mike Leigh is also known for using lengthy improvisation to devise characters, and then films the improvised scenes as his characters encounter new scenarios.

SHORT- AND LONG-FORM IMPROVISATION

Improvisation is usually split into two types: short form and long form. Short-form improv is:

- a series of individual games
- that are (as the name suggests) short – about a maximum of 3–5min each
- in which the game is set and explained in advance and then played

Long-form improv is:

- a series of connected scenes structured in a pre-agreed format
- that are (as the name suggests) collectively long – at least 20min altogether, and anything up to a full-length play
- in which the game is usually discovered by the players, either organically or basing it on something the audience said

Short-form Improv

Short-form improvisation is the performance of already pre-defined games or scene structures developed by Viola Spolin and Keith Johnstone, as set out above. The games played are numerous and always evolving, but many can be found in Keith Johnstone's *Impro* and Viola Spolin's *Improvisation for the Theatre*. There are also some example games given at the end of this book.

Long-form Improv

Long-form improv is the style developed by Del Close and Charna Halpern at IO Theatre, and it gave rise to many incredible formats, including the Harold, the Armando, and Improvised Shakespeare. Other US and now UK theatres also practise long form, such as UCB, Groundlings and The Annoyance. Second City is slightly different in that it hosts a lot of short-form shows and rehearsed revues, where the sketches were developed through an improvisation process.

THE HAROLD

The Harold is often taught in many improv schools that focus on long-form improv because it contains so many of the essential elements of an improv format. You can find out more about the Harold and IO in *Truth in Comedy: The Manual of Improvisation*.

IN SUMMARY			
	Format	**Length**	**Game**
Short form	Games	5min each max	Set and explained in advance
Long form	Scenes	At least 20min collectively	Discovered or invented by players

HAROLD ACT STRUCTURE

Act 1	Group Game	Act 2	Group Game	Act 3
Scene 1		Scene 1		Connections
Scene 2		Scene 2		between Scene 1>
Scene 3		Scene 3		Scene 2> Scene 3

The Harold requires an opener before the team (usually up to seven players) can begin. Typically, a member of the team will ask for a single word from the audience: this inspires a series of monologues, and the team will base their scenes on the material that comes out of those monologues.

The team initiates three scenes, each inspired by the material from the monologue, but all separate. These scenes set the tone and ground the format – they usually establish characters and relationships, and discover the game of the scene (more on that concept later).

To break up each of the acts, some groups run a short-form game also based on the word provided by the audience. These short-form games in between acts can be pre-formatted, and improvised within that, but in most cases they are ambiguous and invented on the spot.

The team then plays Act 2 of their three scenes again – this is a chance to explore the relationship or game they found in the first scene, but this time heightening the stakes, so perhaps in a new location or after time has passed. The second beat can also take a lead character from the first beat and just focus on them, in a new heightened version of the scene.

Then another group game is played.

Finally in Act 3 the scenes are played out again, the relationships and games having been explored to the maximum, and the connections between each of the scenes having been found. This can be done by referring to other characters, or to ideas from the scenes, or the characters can cross scenes and meet each other.

THE ARMANDO

Created by Armando Diaz, a founding member of the Magnet Theatre in New York, this format begins with a monologue from one of the players based on a real event or point of view. The format originally had Armando Diaz delivering the monologues because he was renowned for telling brilliant stories. The team then improvises a series of scenes – separate and connected – on the back of this monologue.

The Armando is a much freer style than the Harold, and gives the team a great deal of freedom to play with editing their scenes. For example, to bring a scene to an end, another player might run across the stage as if to mimic a curtain. And in tagging, a player who is not in a scene taps one of the performing players on the shoulder and takes their place, leaving the other player or players there. He or she could then initiate a brand-new character and scene with those players who remain. The scene is eventually edited, and another monologue begins to inspire some new scenes, not usually based on the same theme, although I have seen improvisers ask for new themes or words. An Armando can be forty minutes long and contains roughly three monologues and three scenes.

The Scene Is What Matters

There are too many formats to mention, but these are the two best known and most widely practised. This is probably because they both represent two approaches so well, the Harold being very structured in devising a format, and the Armando being free flowing. But whatever format you use or watch, it doesn't really matter. Long-form formats are rather like Lego: sometimes it is amusing to follow the instructions and build what is on the box cover, at other times it is fun just to go freestyle. What matters is the basic building block of long-form improv: the scene. The scene is the most basic and critical unit. Get that right – create genuine relationships and grounded games that the audience recognize from their suggestions – and it doesn't really matter what format you use. Just build one scene on the other in any format you like (like Lego).

1
STORYTELLING

What makes a good story? Ask this question to a group of your friends and their answers will probably include 'drama', 'comedy', 'funny characters' or 'something interesting happens'. All these are components of a good story, but what is missing? What always stands out to me is 'detail', because it is the detail that draws in the listener or audience and keeps them interested.

I grew up in a rural town in the west of Ireland, and I have never come across better storytellers than the people I grew up with and who still live in this town. There, a story – any story – contains plenty of detail; it is a tradition that has come from somewhere and has remained. Ask anyone in the local bar what they got up to on Saturday night, and the way the story is woven out is mesmerizing. It'll more than likely begin with what they were doing before they went out, who texted or called them, or what function they had already planned to go to. Then who was in the taxi, who was driving it, and where they were all going – even what they may have been wearing.

By the time they get to the part you were interested in or had talked about, you could have been twenty minutes talking and not been bored, because now you are ready to really understand the story. You know how they were feeling and why they felt that way (you've been given the context to what they were doing earlier and what their frame of mind would have been), and what experiences since leaving home had led them to this point (whom they may have met would have influenced them, whether the person was annoying, or funny, or told a sad story). In short it means that now, you care about the storyteller. You have an insight into why they might have said and done whatever happens next.

From a cultural perspective, and looking at how my background in storytelling shaped my own style, I began thinking of this in terms of improvisation.

IN PRACTICE: THE 'WHO, WHAT, WHERE'

A common approach with beginners in improvisation is almost always to jump straight into the drama and open with an argument, or blaming someone for something, or with a disaster. There is a belief that we need to grab the attention of the audience early and keep them interacting – and if we don't, they will get bored and lose interest. There may be an element of truth in this, but there is a whole series of detail that is missing, and without that the audience won't care.

As soon as the actors step on the stage, the audience have a series of subconscious questions they will need answers for. Who are these characters? Where are they? And what are they doing there? Without knowing who the characters are, where they are in that moment, and without having an idea of what is happening, it can be hard for the audience to connect with the story that is unfolding on the stage. So how do you get round this?

Most improv teachers, schools or actors will advise setting up the 'who', the 'what' and the

Improvised storytelling should start simple and take its time drawing in the audience. The audience gives the suggestions for the story, so start simple: as here, the actors are starting this story in a steady space.

'where'. Even in the stories we share with each other, we always start with setting the scene: for example, 'I was on my way to work this morning and as I approached the bus stop, I saw a police car suddenly speed around the corner.' Without some context building it can be hard for the audience to get into the story.

If we look at the journey of the hero or protagonist in a story, we see that the story starts in their ordinary: today is a normal day for our hero(es). Now this does not have to be boring. A normal day for a pirate would have a lot of things happening that would not happen for an office worker. If our hero is from a mythical or alien

ABOVE: We have a focal point here for both actors as they are working with an external point off the stage. It is the agreement between them that is drawing in the audience.

BELOW: One actor makes a choice to drive the story forwards with a physical offer; at this point the actors should be aware of the audience, and know when to pick up the pace of the story.

A strong physical sign from an actor. However, this could be too soon, and could derail the story. Improvisers should always try to stay aware of where they are in the story so they can continue to bring the audience along.

ABBREVIATED STORYLINE

Opening	Raise the stakes	Blockers	Action	Supporting actors	Achievement	Ending
Normal day of protagonist(s)	Dream or aspiration	Obstacle to overcome	Overcome obstacle	Hero allies	Obstacle is overcome/ dreams realized	A new normal

place, we still need to see what 'ordinary' life is like on any given day.

In *Star Wars* we first meet Luke Skywalker working on his uncle's farm and carrying out the daily chores he would usually get on with on a day-to-day basis. Even though Luke as a character has his own aspirations – which we learn through the dialogue – nothing really happens to him until he meets his mentor and the stakes are raised. The fact that he aspires to higher goals is part of his character background, something we will explore in Chapter 6, Making the Audience Care.

Also keep in mind that a mundane day for one person can be a break in routine for another. Thus a normal day for a firefighter is saving lives, but this is an extraordinary day for the person they rescue. The ordinary day of a brain surgeon is performing an extraordinary skill, yet this is a far from ordinary day for the patient. Understanding who our protagonist is, and how they behave while living their 'normal', is a big part of storytelling.

In improv, using the full journey made by the hero may be too much for actors to follow and keep track of, even though it is not impossible. To keep the story simple, I keep an abbreviated version in my head to keep track of where the storyline is.

Beginners should remember the notion of incorporating these elements into their improvised story. The difficulty lies in avoiding the quick win or early disaster to get the audience interested, because without knowing the normality of the main characters, the audience will quickly lose interest. As a teacher, I see this a lot. If the story is a bank

Players making offers to each other of who they are or what their relationship is, need to be clear so their scene partner can play along.

robbery, students go straight in with a shoot-out, or if it is a romantic day on a yacht they go straight in with a shark attack.

Avoiding the quick win or early disaster can be a good way of getting players to see the value of the normal in the scene. Players with more experience will see the big offer as a normal day for some extraordinary person, and will play that.

With the bank robbery scene, if the robbers rob banks regularly this could be their 'normal' – but they would still need to plan the robbery, which could be a more interesting way of opening a story like this. This way we would find out who they are, why they need the money and where the robbery will take place, as well as where the hideout is.

In the shark scene, the extraordinary character is most likely to be the shark – a shark attack is an extraordinary experience for anyone, but for a shark it is mundane. In *Jaws*, once the shark had figured out that a beach was an easy hunting ground, this became its daily routine.

The key is to normalize the scene, to find the day-to-day. This is also known as the 'who', the 'what' and the 'where'.

Establishing the 'Who'

To newer players, informing the audience as to who the characters are might seem to be a strange task, but it is one that improvisers get to very early in a scene. The 'who' in this case really investigates the relationship between the characters – that is, who they are to each other. They could be strangers

Players making offers for the 'what' of a scene generally use an activity.

meeting for the first time, but this scenario tends to lead to too much conversation in a scene, and ends up being a series of questions back and forth. A scene generally works better when the characters know each other and have a history. When working with beginners in improvisation, this is the scenario I would recommend.

New players feel this is not a good way of telling the audience who they are in the scene, and this makes them feel uncomfortable. A statement such as 'my older brother' or 'my lovely wife of ten years' feels too much – and they are right, it is. But it is a great starting point, and a way to get used to the logistics of the 'who'.

In time, players learn to condense this information into a more subtle sentence and offer more generic lines, such as 'Dad, it's nice to be fishing again', or 'Thanks for dinner, Mum', which keeps things mundane yet gives some detail to your scene partner. You can also make these offers more interesting, such as 'Doctor, I just left the recovery room, our patient with the tonsillitis is comfortable, and it looks as if they'll be fine.' Or 'Would you like a coffee, captain, before we get ready to make our descent into Heathrow?' The key is to present the scene as a normal day in the life of these people, and if possible start at an even level of energy.

Establishing the 'What'

The 'what' is usually the first thing that new players want to get to, as being the piece that they think the audience will find most interesting. Arguably it

Players making offers for the 'where' may point out or use an object to indicate where they are, such as an object in a supermarket or garden.

is, but as stated before, if you jump to it too quickly the audience won't know who or where the players are. And as we see in the examples given above, sometimes the 'what' can get embedded in the 'who', as in the line above, 'Dad, it's nice to be fishing again': this clearly gives us the 'what', namely a person and their dad fishing again after some time.

Establishing the Where

Opening a scene with a disaster or a highly dramatic offer may seem interesting, and may give the actors the impression that the audience are immediately engaged. And it may indeed do that, but without some detail on *who* we are looking at, the audience may be unclear and may subsequently lose interest in the story. So first, let the audience know who they are looking at, what the names of the characters are, and how they know each other. Are they siblings, friends, colleagues, mortal enemies or lovers? How does the audience work this out? The actors must tell them in dialogue.

The actors need to know specifically where they are:

- At home? Whose home, and in what room?
- In a supermarket? Which one? Which aisle?
- In a space station? Where is it orbiting? Make it up!
- In a cowboy saloon, what is it called?
- And what is happening today, why are they there?

Most novice improvisers find the practice of explaining the 'who', 'what' and 'where' to the audience too contrived and unnatural. A very common response to this in a classroom situation is 'People would never speak like this' – to which my reply is always: 'This isn't real life, we are acting and storytelling. We have a responsibility to give the audience this information up front, otherwise they won't know who the characters are and won't care about them.'

THE 'WHO', 'WHAT', 'WHERE' DEFINED

Who: drives the characters

Where: drives the storyline

What: drives the plot

When improvising you can open with a physical offer; it doesn't always have to be verbal. It can also buy time for everyone involved to settle into the scene and buy time to think.

Joining the scene can also be done slowly. Body language is an essential tool for conveying a character point of view; we can see by the actors' demeanour that this character is looking for something, and this will keep the audience engaged.

You can also give them an example of how a 'who', 'what' and 'where' appears in scripted dialogue from any of your favourite television programmes or films (*see* Chapter 9, Teaching, Coaching and Directing).

Whatever example you look at, you should see this information shared with the audience, as it settles them into the story.

Cowboy Example

Imagine the word offered from the audience is 'cowboys': the dialogue might proceed as follows:

Actor 1: 'Whiskey!' (Actor 1 may then take the persona of a cowboy-like character, the body language of a cowboy. He struts on to the stage and imagines he has a gun swinging from his hips, and this gives the audience a great visual of the character's attitude. The line 'Whiskey!' is therefore a great offer, as straight away it gives the impression that the characters are in a saloon.)

Actor 2: 'I see you're back in town, Outlaw Jim' (while he pours a whiskey). (Playing the bartender/saloon owner, Actor 2 would take the attitude of the owner, which would be of lower status, but would still command a lot of social respect, so he wouldn't be afraid to stand his ground in his own establishment.)

Engagement between the characters can be fed from the dialogue; there is never any need to rush the exchanging of objects, nor the exercise of feeding off each other's body language and energy.

Actor 1: 'Leave the bottle!'

Actor 2: 'Now, Jim…'

Actor 1: (interrupts) 'I *said*, leave the bottle, O'Malley!'

Actor 2: 'We don't want no trouble here Jim, you hear! River Creek is a peaceful town, and the Thirsty Horse Saloon ain't seen a gunfight for six weeks now.'

So, in as few as six lines, what do we now know?

- The physicality of the characters gives us an insight into their social standing and relationship (more on this in Chapter 4, Spontaneity and Listening, and Chapter 6, Making the Audience Care).
- One is called Outlaw Jim, so implies a character typical of a rough gun-slinging cowboy.
- The saloon owner's name is O'Malley. It can be useful to give each other names, as this helps with the robustness of the scene.
- The characters clearly know each other.

Objects should be accepted if offered; even if the actor is not sure what it is, he can invent something.

- The last time Jim was there, there was an incident.
- Jim likes to drink whiskey.
- The town is called River Creek.
- The saloon is called the Thirsty Horse Saloon.
- The six lines as outlined in the cowboy example would take less than ten seconds to deliver.

The audience will take in all this information, and this solid beginning will give them and the actors a platform on which to build the story.

Note: In this example I have added stage directions for reference, but these are, of course, also improvised and at the discretion of the actor (*see* Chapter 3, Using Your Body and the Space). There is also the option of side coaching, which the director can do to help the actors in a rehearsal space (*see* Chapter 8, Coaching, Teaching and Directing).

The simple statements in the cowboy example therefore set a visual for the audience and give both actors plenty to play with. They also give any supporting actors in the wings plenty of material with which they can add colour: maybe the local gang shows up, or the sheriff, or to be even more creative and set the scene, maybe a few extras appear and just simply play cards in the background. Or even simpler, background actors can enter as extras and be saloon girls, or card-playing cowboys. Whatever it is, now the scene is set. The audience want to see what happens next, to know how this will play out – but no one knows yet, not even the actors.

Estate Agent Example

Creating a cowboy-like character would be reasonably straightforward, as you have a lot to tap into: an accent, an attitude, specific body language. So how would you do it if you were playing an estate agent or a bank clerk? Or an estate agent showing a bank clerk round a property? Open the scene in a simple way:

Actors can join to add colour to the scene; joining actors don't have to add dialogue unless they have something interesting to add to drive the story.

Actor 1: 'And so, as you can see Mr Smith, the property is a typical two-up, two-down terrace. Going for a really good price.'
Actor 2: 'Yes, and Rosewood Avenue is so much nicer than the one you showed me on Baysquinn Road, Jennifer – wow, I love this kitchen!'
Actor 1: 'You have a spare room for when your daughter comes to visit.'
Actor 2: 'Yes, it's been tough on her since her mum and I divorced.'

Again, we have loaded the scene with information on where it could go.

In both situations the actors are taking care to give out as much detail in the opening lines as possible: it's the same as being efficient with the offers you give out. However, at the same time you don't want to overdo it, so give space back to your scene partner (more on this in Chapter 2, Yes, And…). Like a television programme or a film, it starts with a mundane day, because we need to see the characters in their normal lives. If we

The established actors already on stage may have an offer for you, so there is no harm in waiting to see if they engage you.

don't, we won't care about them when the stakes are raised.

In improvisation the scene is set, and the actors and audience are comfortable with who and where everyone is, and a mundane day in the lives of these characters.

TIPS ON SCENE SETTING

- Make a simple opening offer. Don't ask questions, instead make a statement! Asking a question is forcing your scene partner to do the work. Comment on the character's clothes, expression, mood or state of mind.
- Be generous, make them look good. Make other people cool, interesting characters. If they take or assume the high status, then let them have it and play generously.
- Make your statement clear, so they know exactly what your offer is. This means avoid small talk, such as asking how someone is, or where they want to go on holiday.
- Start with a normal day at the office, farm, home or wherever your scene is set. We are looking for 'a day in the life' before the drama or comedy starts.

Actors can raise the stakes either by moving the story into the location they are in, or they can take us to a new location as long as they make it clear where the story has moved to.

The same rules can apply again: once the 'who, what, where' is set up, others can join in.

RAISE THE STAKES

Let's revisit Outlaw Jim and O'Malley in the Thirsty Horse Saloon at River Creek. In this scene, we have a normal day for O'Malley. It would be nothing unusual for a wandering gunslinger to walk into his saloon. For Outlaw Jim, this activity might be less frequent, but still regular enough for it not to be extraordinary.

Once we have a mundane situation in place and we have basic knowledge about the characters, we can now look for ways to raise the stakes. The audience would have some investment at this point, as they are ready for the lead characters to get more interesting.

We know that Jim is back in town after some time, and this is an opportunity for either actor to introduce a reason for his return. The options might include romance, business, to settle a score.

Either actor can make the offer as to why Jim is back in town – it doesn't have to be the actor playing Jim. In fact, it is more improvised if the offer as to why Jim is back comes from the actor playing O'Malley.

O'Malley: 'Sheriff's been asking for ya, said to let him know soon as you made your way back into town!'

Outlaw Jim: 'Well then, you better let him know.'

O'Malley: 'Now Jim, no trouble you hear, cost me $100 to get the place fixed up after last time.'
Outlaw Jim: (Throws gold coins on the bar.) 'Add it to my tab.'
O'Malley: 'Sheriff's still not happy about you courting his sister, and's been heard saying he's gonna get you for something.'
Outlaw Jim: 'He's gotta catch me first!'

In this example, we see the stakes raised for both characters: O'Malley is concerned for the safety of his saloon, and we learn why the sheriff is so keen to see Jim. Also, we have more characters to meet as the actors have introduced them to us: as an audience we are now interested to meet them.

Tips for Raising the Stakes

- The offer could be physical (*see* Chapter 3, Using your Body and the Space).
- Keep it simple, don't try to drive the entire storyline yourself. Play it like a ping-pong match, swap lines.
- Endow the other actor with attributes and an offer of their past. In the cowboy story, Actor 2 (O'Malley) makes the offer of history between Jim and the sheriff. These types of offer are considered generous as they help Actor 1 (Outlaw Jim) indulge more in their character.
- Let your scene partner have an opportunity to make counter offers, so try and be incremental when building on offers.
- Aspirations and/or past events are a great tool for raising the stakes and making the story more interesting – offering these is a better practice than self-endowing them on your own character.

We will explore heightening at greater length in Chapter 5, Finding the Game.

BLOCKERS AND OBSTACLES

At this point in the scene the audience need to see the third character mentioned: the sheriff. If an off-stage character is mentioned, then we must see them. The actor playing O'Malley doesn't have to leave the stage: he can stay and keep up his space work (polishing glasses, wiping down the bar), and add dialogue if and when it might be necessary – but the spotlight must be allowed to fall on the new centrepiece of the story, which is the dialogue between Jim and the sheriff.

At this point the actor playing the sheriff already knows the point of tension between himself (the sheriff) and Jim, which is that he (the sheriff) disapproves of Jim courting his sister – but now we can assume that the audience want to understand why this is. It would be interesting here if the actors explored the history between Jim and the sheriff, as the audience will want to see more than just a 'No just because' reason. A useful tool here can be to pull in a secret between the two main characters, which can be done slowly.

Now that the audience, players and extras all know where and who these characters are, everything else becomes interesting. For students, this is the point where the framework and structure stops, and the creativity and fun between the actors come in. Subsequent offers can now become vaguer as the players begin to negotiate the history and to build the tension between the characters. The following is an example of what could unfold in the scene:

The sheriff comes on stage.

Sheriff: 'Outlaw Jim, I heard you were in back in River Creek!'
Outlaw Jim: 'Got some business to settle.'
Sheriff: 'Business you should have left behind you years ago!'
Outlaw Jim: 'Some things just can't get left that easy, Sheriff.'

This dialogue between the actors is not giving us any more details about the characters, but because we have enough information, we now have room for drama and some creativity to happen between the players. The players can enjoy this, as will the audience, but the players must be careful not to overdo the drama as the audience will get bored.

At this point the players might find a game to play, or we may see the story move on as a narrative.

We will explore more of this plot building in Chapter 2, Yes, And…, and the work of extras in Chapter 5, Finding the Game.

CALLING IN ALLIES

Calling in allies is not an essential part of the story, but it is a great opportunity for extras to make an appearance, and also for colour to be added to the scene. In a traditional hero's journey this is where the hero's new friends or allies join the fight. Or in some cases the hero's quest crosses with that of the friends they meet. Again, with reference to *Star Wars*, these characters would be Han Solo, Princess Leia and the rest of the alliance.

When improvising, the allies could be called in by the hero, or it could be their nemesis, or the actors off-stage could make the offer themselves. It can be a brave call for the extra off-stage to make, as beginners often feel that if they enter the stage, they are disrupting the story. But disruption is good, as is anything that disrupts the status quo – and it could well be that the actors on stage are getting stuck and are silently waiting for one of their teammates to come in and save them.

Staying with our cowboy scene, we have a situation where the main characters are in a potential Mexican stand-off (no pun intended here) and could be stuck in the route they have taken. Extras who might enter could be:

• O'Malley the barman
• The sheriff's sister (as yet to be named)

• An unmet or unmentioned person

Best practice would say that bringing on a person whose existence we know about is less confusing for the audience, particularly if the players are running a narrative. However, if they are playing a game, then a new character could be the right move – see Chapter 5, Finding the Game.

In our cowboy scene O'Malley re-enters (or stops his space work), and the dialogue might continue as follows:

O'Malley: 'Best leave it lie, sheriff, Jim ain't got no trouble to cause.'
Sheriff: 'I'm the law here, and I'll be the judge of that.'
O'Malley: 'Best may be you was moving on, Jim – River Creek ain't got nothing for you no more.'
Outlaw Jim: 'I's come here for business to settle.'

Enter the sheriff's sister (as yet unnamed).

Sister: 'James!'
Outlaw Jim: (Removing his hat.) 'Bernadette! Well, it's good to see you! You is looking…'
Sheriff: 'Leave it there, Jim.'
Outlaw Jim: 'Now don't you tell me how to speak…'
Bernie: 'Jim, there is something I need to tell you…'
Outlaw Jim: 'I ain't here to cause trouble, I's just asking you to come with me… to San Francisco, let's start again, leave this two-horse town behind us.'
Bernie: 'I can't Jim, I just…'
Outlaw Jim: 'Bernie, come with me. I came back for you.'

O'Malley moves towards Bernie and puts his arm around her waist.

Bernie: 'I couldn't wait Jim, I just…'
O'Malley: 'It's OK, Bernie.'

Outlaw Jim: 'You mean… Why, you no good (to O'Malley) dirty… I thought you were my friend.'

Obstacle is Overcome/ Dreams Realized (or Not)

In this part of the story we see either an up- or a downturn for our hero(es). There is tension built. For ease of explanation I'll stay with our story of Outlaw Jim. So far we know that Jim has returned to River Creek to find his old girlfriend and run away with her to San Francisco. However, two things are blocking this:

- His love interest is the sheriff's sister, Bernie, and the sheriff has a problem with their relationship (we do not know why).
- His old friend O'Malley the saloon owner and Bernie have started a relationship.

What will happen next is unknown to all, both actors and audience. In this love triangle both men would presumably fight for the interest of Bernie, and the actor playing Bernie can play this drama and tension. One could argue that the finale of the scene lies with the character Bernie, but one of the antagonists could also shoot Jim, though this would be somewhat unsatisfactory for the audience.

Find an Ending/ A New Normal

Depending on the type of improvised scene you have just experienced, the options of how to end can come in different ways. If you are running a dramatic or realistic scene, the end can come with a natural resolution to the story.

In our cowboy story, we could play it out in a simple fashion where the scene ends in a shoot-out between the sheriff and Outlaw Jim and O'Malley. At this point any of the characters could close the story with a short narrative, playing it as if the entire scene were a reminiscence: in the past they had witnessed this shoot-out between Outlaw

Jim, the sheriff and O'Malley, and the scene they have enacted is a recollection of this event. Or the actors might go down a more comic route, and all four could go to San Francisco to start a new life.

Whatever it is, to make the story complete we need to see a change and a new normal for at least the main character.

Whatever choice the actors make to end the story, it is up to the other players and/or the MC to make the call at the right time, and close it.

SUMMARY

- Start simple.
- Don't make it complicated.
- Say yes to the obvious.
- Let the audience lead you (they usually hint to where they want the story to go, so pay attention to them).
- The hero's journey is a template, and may or may not be helpful, depending on the type of scene you are in.
- Pay attention to any patterns or games that arise (*see* Chapter 5, Finding the Game).

The ending can be on a dramatic note, when it just feels right to end.

- Go full circle, so have the ending bring us back to the point where we started.
- End by death, where the tension finally erupts and one character explodes and attacks the other; this can then be called by the MC. Also, a gun or some other weapon may have been brought on stage, and if you bring a gun on stage, you need to use it.
- Break the fourth wall, where one character turns to the audience and addresses them directly, saying something like, 'Well, I wasn't expecting that, were you?'
- Worlds align, so a grounded character may give up and join the surreal world they are trapped in; or vice versa, and the surreal character becomes grounded (see Chapter 5, Finding the Game).

- Stop it in time; either you or the MC should be aware of how to live edit (we'll come back to this).
- Find a closing button.
- Once the edit or ending is called either by you or the MC, leave the stage.

EXERCISES

Story Die

- When running the exercise make sure that players move the story onwards every time.
- Have players make the characters act and do things – avoid speaking about the character's thoughts..
- Make sure the players keep focused on a central story.

Seanchaí

- Uses narrative along with acting to blend a story.
- Helps avoid repetition.
- It forces players to add to the narrative, and not show just what's been said by the narrator.
- The narrator needs to give the players more open-ended leads to add to, as this helps build tension.

EVERYDAY LIFE

Presentations: Use a storytelling template to relay your message: this is a great way to show a story of where you were, what you did, and where you are now.

- Where we were, where we are and where we are going
- Think of this when presenting a product, an idea or a project. Executive leaders like to know why the project is in its current state, how it got there, what we have learnt so far, and where and how we plan to get to the next phase. All typical storytelling aspects.
- There is also an opportunity for the presenter to use a real-life story as an analogy to drive home their point: this engages the audience.
- In any story, the protagonists have a learning journey, so by the end of the story they have a new perspective on life. Ending on a high note with key takeaways (the new norm) is how a presenter would do this when using a storytelling template for business.

Social storytelling: Recounting an experience or event: the best social storytellers give you a fully rounded story with a beginning, a middle and an end.

2
YES, AND...

The most famous improvisation pillar of all is 'Yes, and…'

'Yes, and…' is the principal take-away transferable skill often used by those who have taken improvisation classes into their personal and professional lives. This is because it has a built-in collaborative element that gives people who become familiar with it a method of not blocking an idea or suggestion given to them by another person in any aspect of life, whether work, personal or social. It also opens the door for a conversation on any topic, even if you are not an expert; it encourages people to listen with proper intent.

Before exploring this concept, let's examine what 'Yes, and…' means. A common starting point for beginners who are trying to understand the concept of 'yes, and…' is just to say 'yes', thinking that this may be enough. In fact, it's easy to say 'yes' and not add anything, when the important part is the 'and…'!

What is very often seen amongst beginners is that the 'and…' is turned into a question, which means the work is given back to the partnering actor. The common misconception here with beginners is that by asking this question they think they are helping by being conversational, whereas in fact this causes the scene to get stuck. An audience is not very interested in a conversation where a series of questions are asked and answered, like two friends having a catch-up or strangers meeting for the first time. Instead they want to see two actors take on characters, and build on the situation they are in by adding to each offer played.

Every improviser has a responsibility to make life easier for those around them, and the easiest way to do this is always to try and give something back to your scene partner. Endow them somehow, or give them a piece of valuable information about their character.

Remember nobody on the stage knows where the story will end up, so we all need to do our best to give input. Don't get caught in the idea that the extroverted or outgoing person in your class – the one who can always think of something to say – has all the answers.

The easiest way to think about it is to imagine that 'Yes, and…' is like the cement and bricks when building a wall. On top of the already laid bricks, a builder adds a layer of cement – this is the 'Yes' – then they add the next line of bricks, which is the 'and', and the wall is now higher. However, before the additional line of bricks is added, the builder must make sure that the layer of cement is compacted and ready to take the new line of bricks. If the cement is applied with little attention, it will not hold the next line safely and the wall will eventually become unsteady and fall.

The same applies to using 'Yes, and…' in an improv sense. It is easy to say 'Yes' and not really pay attention to what your scene partner has said. If this happens, then there is a chance that your addition may not fit, and you start to build an unsteady scene.

Keeping each line incremental to the conversation or story is a very effective way of ensuring that the scene will hold together. This can be tricky, as people new to improv are inclined to make the

The meaning of 'Yes, and…' is to accept any offer you get; offers are gifts from other improvisers and should be accepted and added to – it can be a physical or verbal offer, even an object, and should be accepted with glee.

BELOW: Starting in the middle of the scene can develop a quick basis for characters; an object of interest can be a great way to open.

'Yes, and...' a big jump just to make the scene seem interesting. This is not necessary. Short, simple, firm additions are more effective and give the audience time to stay with you. Let the scene play like this and you will find the inspirational theme that the scene will cling to and run with (more on this in Chapter 5, Finding the Game).

The important point to remember here is to allow the conversation to flow, and to try not to force a situation or outcome.

There is nothing wrong with entering a scene with an opening idea or even a rough thread to fall back on; moreover as you play with regular players you tend to learn how to follow some people, and to know at the top of the scene if they are driving a theme or story, or negotiating the outcome. Both can be valid, but for true 'Yes, and...' it works better if players swap statements with additions.

IN PRACTICE

A concept I share with students is to think about editing in a more definitive way. When you watch a film, you don't always see the two characters turn up at the restaurant and exchange small talk before they get down to business – unless of course it is part of the story of how these characters meet. There are many scenes in *The Sopranos*, for example, where we cut straight to the office behind 'the Bing' where the characters are already in mid-meeting and conversation, and in minimal time we are getting to the crux of why they are there.

Start in the Middle

Look at any long-running 'soap' (*EastEnders*, *Home and Away*, *Offspring*) and you would probably find that if you were to join in at any point and in any season, you would fairly quickly get to know who everyone was and what was happening in their lives. This is because the characters get to the story point directly and avoid small talk – or in other words, the story is edited.

When watching a film called *Inception* by Christopher Nolan, one scene caught my interest. The main protagonist, Cobb – played by Leonardo DiCaprio – explains how in a dream, a situation always starts in the middle: you create and discover at the same time: you never remember how you got to the situation, only that you are there. If you wake up and remember you dreamt you were in a hotel, you don't have any memory of how you got to the hotel, or of having a shower, getting ready, leaving the house, commuting there or arriving there. You simply start the dreamt experience at a certain point.

An improvised scene can be started in the same way: there is no need to explain how the characters got there in the first place – this can be ironed out later if required, or become part of the story.

To summarize this notion, when you improvise you create, discover and *perform* all at the same time, making improvisation a very real and raw art form. With no preparation on what our topics will be, we respond in the moment.

So to begin with, try not to worry about where the story may be going. Instead think about where you are right now: where you are, and why you are there. The stronger the offer, the easier it is for the other actor to add to it. The difference here, of course, is that as it is not scripted, the actors have no idea where they may be going, and this is where the 'Yes, and…' comes into play.

Let's start with the notion that any idea is a good idea. And when we improvise, we hold that true to all offers. There is always a way to make them work. In the previous chapter (Chapter 1, Storytelling) we looked at opening a scene, and how a mundane day in the life of the characters is always a good starting block. 'Yes, and…' will then play into building on this.

If starting from the middle, an actor may lead with some dialogue; this is also useful to establish a 'who, what, where'.

The most effective way to make a 'Yes, and...' work is to follow a simple pattern:

- Clarify what has just been said to you: you can either repeat it out loud, or do it silently in your head – either way make sure you are clear on what the offer is to you.
- Find a way to confirm what just been said: if the opening offer was 'It's very wet out today', the confirmation could be 'Yes, I brought my umbrella!'
- The 'and...' could be simple: 'We can share it while we wait for the bus.'

The best way to make the 'Yes, and...' effective is to make it incremental. Make small steps when adding to each offer. For example, if the scene starts in a kitchen and the next line is that it is the kitchen of an army base, this is technically a decent 'Yes, and...'. However, it could put some restrictions on the rest of the scene, as it is quite a jump. If the journey of information to the fact that the characters are in an army base were more incremental, the scene would be more improvised as the outcome is more negotiated. It also makes the scene more enjoyable for the audience.

OPENING A SCENE

To practise your 'Yes, and...' a good habit is to apply a confirmation step to the process: 'Yes, *confirm*, and...' For example, if the opening offer is verbal, it could have some information in it about where or who the characters are. And to make it incremental, a good tip is to say the obvious. For example:

Actor 1: 'Will you have a cup o' tea, Dad?'
Actor 2: 'Oh, I'd love a cup o' tea, one sugar please. And after the tea, we'll get the decking finished.'

At this point the dialogue tells us that a person and their father are finishing work being done on some decking. However, we are not sure where exactly, although the feeling is that it is one of their homes – though whose home we are not sure yet. The assumption could be made that we are in the home of the person offering the refreshment, but at the same time it would not be unusual for a person to feel at home in their parents' house, considering that they may even have grown up there. However, this could be an offer to buy tea in a café. The 'where' is still open.

Usually for beginners, good practice is to close this loop and confirm the location to allow the story to continue; for example:

Actor 1: 'Yes, it would be great to get it done before Mum gets home from work.'
(Where it is confirmed.)

However, more experienced actors may decide to play it out some more and see what happens, as in:

Actor 1: 'Yes, it would be great to have it finished before the weekend, so we can have a barbecue.' (Exactly where is still open.)

Beginners to improvisation tend to find this unnatural, but the point is to get into the habit of securing this information. More experienced players allow the conversation to flow, and try not to force a situation or outcome. What could happen is that one of the actors has a fully formed idea in their head of where they want the story to go. If they are not getting the response they want from their scene partner, then the 'Yes, and...' turns into 'No, but...', and if the other player doesn't give way, the scene will become stuck.

There is nothing wrong with entering a scene with an opening idea or even a rough thread to fall back on, and as you play with regular people as part of a troupe you tend to learn how to follow some people, and know at the top of the scene if they are driving a theme or story, or negotiating the outcome. Both can be valid, but for true 'Yes, and...' it is always better to treat it like a ping-pong match. To make it simple, use a pattern:

Offer – accept – confirm – 'Yes, and...' – while at the start of a scene working out the 'who, what, where' and using 'Yes, and...' to get there.

Example Scene

The audience suggestion is 'Research'.

Actor 1: 'Professor, I see it there just a hundred yards ahead.'

The following things should be considered when you get an offer:

- What tone did the other actor use: have they handed me the high status, or are we peers, or are they the higher status?
- What is the obvious response here?
- How can I follow the pattern?

The first option is to accept the offer of professor, and the 'what' you may be looking at:

'Yes, I see it. It's beautiful!' (Accept.) How amazing to see it in its natural habitat! (Confirmation.) And I never would have done it without the help of the most experienced ranger in the country!' (And this 'Yes, and...' also gives the other actor a character.)

This passes the baton back to the other actor, and with open opportunity, as we are still not sure where these characters are (although it seems they are looking at a creature in its natural habitat):

'We are lucky, professor, to see the snow leopard – ghosts of the mountain the locals call them. It's getting dark, professor; we should return to camp before the temperature drops any more.'

The scene could now continue as to why the professor is there, and how they met, and what other adventures these two characters have been on before. Or in a simpler scene, what is so special about this snow leopard? Does the professor or the ranger have a history with this snow leopard?

All these options are open for the actors to call on, but the important thing to remember is to continue to make statements that bring more information, which is the 'Yes, and...'.

This can seem rather intimidating for the improvisers, especially for beginners, as there is a lot to do and pay attention to. A visual learner might like to think of it in table format:

Revisiting our scene about the estate agent from Chapter 1:

Actor 1: 'And so, as you can see Mr Smith, it is a typical two-up, two-down terrace. Going for a really good price.'
Actor 2: 'Yes, and Rosewood Avenue is so much nicer than the one you showed me on Baysquinn Road, Jennifer – *wow*, I love this kitchen!'
Actor 1: 'You have a spare room for when your daughter comes to visit.'
Actor 2: 'Yes, it's been tough on her since her mum and I divorced.'

In this opening the first line adheres to the 'who, what, where' rule by naming the other character and giving an idea of where they are. This is an example of opening in the middle of the scene, removing all the small talk that this type of relationship would normally start with. The

BRICK–CEMENT–BRICK

Opening	*Agreeing and confirming*	*Adding the 'and...'*	*Repeat*
Start in the middle of a scene	Take the offer, confirm it. This helps the actors really listen to each other	The 'and...' should be built off the confirmation, not the 'Yes'. Adding to the 'Yes' can be weak and does not always add to the story	Repeat this process until you are happy with the foundation of the story

An open type of activity gives other players many options to add to it; your opening action or line is an offer, so let others join in to build on it. In this example the joining improviser decides to copy the opening activity. Here the 'Yes, and...' may be a verbal offer as to the type of activity they are doing.

Unless the improviser who makes the offer justifies it, it can be preserved as anything that would make a good 'Yes, and...' from any other improviser.

Other improvisers can enter and make offers if the scene needs it.

solid opening gives us the impression that these characters have met before, and therefore they have some personal information on each other. The 'Yes, and…' from Actor 2 tells us that, and the 'and…' confirms their specific location in London, and specifically in what room they are in.

This information may seem trivial, and a lot of beginners think, well what's the point of knowing that? But it is another piece of information that can be used, or not, later in the scene. We then quickly find out that Actor 2 (Mr Smith) is divorced and has a daughter. And if you consider the scene more closely, you will see that the information is exchanged as opposed to being self-endowed.

Being Generous with Offers

It is easier for fellow actors to build on the offers they are given if these are loaded with opportunities. Going back to the scene about the snow leopard, with beginners such a scene might play out like this:

Ranger: 'What is so interesting about the snow leopard to you, professor?'
Professor: 'Well, when I was a young boy I saw one in the zoo and thought, I need to know more about these amazing animals.'
Ranger: 'I loved the zoo too, it's what made me want to be a wildlife ranger.'

Now, this dialogue is decent and could work if we let it play out, but each character is endowing themselves: they are explaining to us why they are where they are. And although they may make sense from a conversational point of view, this is not what we are doing. To make the experience easier for the other actor, a good strategy is to endow them – to give them a gift of information about each other, and to make it relevant to the situation they are in now. For example:

Ranger: 'We are lucky, professor, to see the snow leopard – ghosts of the mountain the locals call them. It's getting dark, professor; we should return to camp before the temperature drops any more.'

Professor: 'Yes, good idea. We have an early start tomorrow as I really need to get to the second location by sunrise.'

Ranger: 'The team will be at the camp soon with the additional equipment you requested.'

The idea with each of these offers is that there is something in the statement that the other actor can pick up on and use to drive the story – the story being what is happening now, and less about the history of the characters. The statement that they are lucky to see a snow leopard gives the other actor something to build on, instead of having to work to answer the question.

MAKING MISTAKES

From time to time it may happen that one or other of the actors mishears or misinterprets an offer. Also they may not understand, and may choose to go their own way. Regarding mistakes, bear in mind the following:

- Making a mistake is a gift, and the offer should always be taken and built on, so be sure to 'Yes, and...' it.
- Try to avoid correcting the mistake.
- Calling out the mistake is fine: it shows the audience you are listening, and it looks more improvised when you run with it.
- The audience would have heard/seen the mistake too, and are more interested in your building on it than correcting it, as this comes across more as real improv.

One improviser might make a physical offer, which could be there to help them figure out on the spot where to go with the story next.

In support, the other improviser can copy to help buy time and build on it.

GIVING THE OTHER ACTOR SPACE

The opening offer could be physical, so watch out for this (more in Chapter 3, Using Your Body and the Space). At the start of a scene, your partner may enter with an opening idea, and this could be a physical offer too. Even if you have no idea of what the other actor is doing, leave them the space to act it out, and try not to snatch it from them.

If you do snatch it, or if an idea with which you open physically is snatched from you, the best way to deal with it is to run with the new offer. Experienced and generous improvisers will do this and not hold a grudge. It is important to remember to run with the first offer.

Example of Giving Your Partner Space

In a recent *Livewired* show, we ran a longer multi-scene piece following a one-word suggestion from the audience (not the Harold). Their suggestion was 'origin', and my scene partner came on stage with a slightly scooped body shape. Of course, I had no idea what she was up to, so I mirrored it (this was my acceptance of the opening physical offer). I knew she had more to offer, so I continued to give her the space as I waited for her opening line of dialogue. This was 'Husband, today I build fire!'

Immediately I understood that her 'take' on the audience's suggestion was 'The origin of the species', so I followed the pattern with the reply 'Wife! (the confirmation) I bring animal kill, so we can put on fire to cook!' (the 'And...')

The scene continued to be no more than a domestic scene between a cave-dwelling couple. No dinosaur, or meteors, or anything drastic needed to happen, as the audience were sufficiently engaged with the domestic life of pre-historic man.

Continuing with our 'Yes, and...', the scene eventually evolved into us becoming the first ever monogamous couple, when again, nothing drastic needed to happen. It was just a simple story involving two people, and by adding to the story between us in an incremental way, the audience came with us and were on board the whole way, even empathizing with the characters as they saw a simple love story played out in an unknown time.

Had I not followed the other actor and given her space to see what her idea was, I would have blocked her physical offer. Unfortunately this is something that often happens. Even in live shows experienced improvisers will see a physical offer from their scene partner, and instead of allowing them some space to let them play it out a little further, they jump in with a 'Yes, and...' The scene can still work in a different way, but if this is done too often by an improviser they may gain a reputation for being aggressive and ungenerous.

AVOID OVERLOADING THE SCENE

Overloading the scene with too many offers means that one actor throws several ideas at the other actor. For example, they may offer who they are, where they are right now, and what is happening at this moment in their lives. In other words, they take full ownership of the 'who, what, where'.

This is a lot for the other actor to take on in one go, and they may only respond to one of the offers and not fully remember all the other information thrown at them. It also takes some of the fun away from the other actor, who then doesn't have the opportunity to give input into the story. It is always better to treat it like a ping-pong match and allow

The reply of 'No' may be a way of saying 'Yes' to the storyline or scene: if you are in a dramatic scene, it may be necessary to say 'no' in order to drive forwards the confrontation or point of view of your character.

each actor to apply the 'Yes, and…'; in this way information is fed gently both to the actors and to the audience.

SAYING 'NO' IN A SCENE

Is it ever all right to say 'no' in a scene? The short answer is yes, it is. Nevertheless it is a reasonably intermediate to advanced move, and should only be applied if the actors know what they are doing. The following are some things you need to be aware of before doing this:

- If the scene is plot driven, then this needs to be reasonably established for the 'no' to work. This means that if there is a conflict between two characters, a 'no' is required in the dialogue to enable the disagreement.
- If the scene is a pattern or game, then the 'no' may be part of the game (more on finding the game in Chapter 5).
- The actor saying 'no', and the actor receiving it, need to be aware of what could be happening: it may be a game being cultivated in the scene, or it is plot driven.

The danger of saying 'no' for beginners is that it tends to be the gateway to an argument in a scene. Beginners tend to look for the dramatic, and the easy route into this is to start an argument. Conflict is a piece of theatre we see all the time, from Shakespearean plays to *EastEnders*, which gives the impression of being good theatre.

The important thing to remember is that it is a tool used by the playwrights to drive the story, as each character is predefined and has their own arc. This means that the conflict is positioned at a point in a play in order that some underlying secret will be revealed, or to reveal something about, or to, the protagonist or antagonist.

What happens in an improvised scene (unless it is predefined by a director) is that everyone wants to be the hero and win the argument. And because the dialogue is improvised, no one can ever be wrong. So what happens is that this type of scene spirals and goes nowhere.

To make it work, the improvisers tend to be experienced, and to know when to give way. A few decisions need to be made on the spot, such as:

- What is this story about?
- Who is the hero?
- How can I give way to make them look good?

One of the actors will then make an offer, which will be to stand down. The other actor will then pick up on that offer and the plot can move on.

Example of Saying 'No' in a Scene

In a recent *Livewired* show, our characters were a father and his son. The father (played by myself) played a simple offer of encouraging his son to join him in the family business, albeit with a stern tone. The young actor playing the son showed resistant agreement: this meant that although he played along with the offer of the dutiful son, his body language and tone – which were signals to his partner of his character choice as an actor – were that the character of the son was not fully in agreement with the idea of joining the family business.

The actors were therefore agreeing with the drama that would follow, and the story of this disagreement of the characters.

In the second scene in this story, the son reveals to the father that he has aspirations of his own and wants to leave home and study to be a graphic designer. The actors' next decision was to make the call on which storyline was more interesting to the audience. The scene developed into an emotional argument between these characters, where the word 'No' was frequently used by both.

As this was a typical template of a coming-of-age story, I made the call in my head that it would give the audience more satisfaction to see the younger character have his dreams come through. My next offer to my scene partner was therefore to show him the signs of my character arc, to show that the father understood that his son has dreams of his own. Again both of us were back on the same page regarding the arc of the story, and we were able to play this out in slow dramatic fashion, knowing that the scene would end with the father giving his son his blessing.

As characters, we used the word 'no' a lot, especially during the dramatic high points of the scene – but as actors we were in fact saying 'yes' to the plot and to each other because we had found an agreement on the story arc.

This can take some time to get, and usually works better with improvisers who know each other, as they can pick up on each other's subtleties. Experienced improvisers who are not familiar with each other can also do this – it just takes a little more attention to character and storyline, and deciding which character is giving way to drive that story.

SUMMARY

- Follow this pattern: accept – confirm – and.
- Make a statement and avoid questions.
- Stay in the real world, at least at the start, and be obvious.
- Allow mistakes to be a gift.
- Give space to your fellow actors.
- Try not to overload your scene partner with too many offers at once.
- Using 'no' can work, if it drives the plot or game.

EXERCISES

Random statements:

- Take a partner, decide who is A and B.
- Face each other.
- A: Name a random object: 'I have a cup of tea.'
- B: 'Yes, you have a cup of tea, it's our break time; and after tea we will get back on the road.'
- A: 'Yes, after tea we will get back on the road, cover another couple of hundred miles, and get to London before 6pm.'

Freeze tag:

Use this exercise to say 'yes' to the scene you have just begun. Make sure the other player knows what your offer is as soon as possible, so they can 'Yes, and…' too.

Offer a gift:

- Player A offers Player B a gift and tells them what it is: 'I've got a grandfather clock for you.'
- Player B must except the gift with as much glee as possible, and justify exactly why it is important to them. 'And…' should be a story, and not that they will just use it, or that it will look good in their home – for example, they could say 'A grandfather clock, this is a great gift and important to me because when I was young if I couldn't sleep my mother would tell me to listen to the tick, tock of the grandfather clock in the hall that I could hear from my bedroom, and the soothing sound helped me fall asleep. Now that my job is getting very stressful and is keeping me awake at night I can listen again to the clock making its sounds, and it will help me sleep. Which is important because I need lots of sleep to do a good job at work.'

EVERYDAY LIFE

- When having a conversation with your friends, family or significant others, try saying 'Yes, and…' to their ideas, and build on that. So if your friend says 'Let's get a drink on Friday', follow it up with 'Yes, let's do that, and head to the cinema and see the new film that is out.'
- In a work situation saying 'Yes, and…' to an idea from a colleague is a great way to build a collaborative environment in your workplace.
- 'Yes, and…' is very useful in brainstorming with a group of people when planning an activity.

3
USING YOUR BODY AND THE SPACE

It is important that improvisers use the space around them. Engaging an audience and bringing them into your world can be challenging, so we need to give them as much detail as we can to draw them in. We are asking the audience to use their imaginations and come with us on a journey, and we do this without costume, script or props. All that improvisers have is their body language and the space on the stage, so they must make the most of this.

The audience is always on your side. This means that if you show them you are holding a cup of tea, they will believe you are holding a cup of tea. Their 'mind's eye' will put it there, and you must keep this consistent or you will break the illusion.

To begin with, you can move around the stage. Own it: avoid walking nervously and hoping it'll all work out – rather, stride on with confidence and look as if you know what you are doing. Of course, we know that nerves may get to you, especially when you are starting out, as this is undoubtedly a scary thing to do. So, fill the awkward silence and do something. The stage is yours.

This means using the space by adding mime techniques to embellish the world in which the characters currently find themselves. The improviser is in complete control of where they are, and can add and remove objects to and from the space as they see fit. It is very common for improvisers to stand in one spot, and this looks exactly how it sounds: two people standing on a stage, and you should try to avoid this.

Moving around and using the stage also prevents improvisers from being simply 'talking heads',

and keeps them grounded in the scene or game. As described in Chapter 2 ('Yes, And…'), when opening a scene there are several things they need to do to get set up – and while their brain is busy figuring these things out, their external appearance should give the impression that they know exactly what is going on. This is part of the 'I know what I am doing' illusion they are selling to the audience, and is done by miming actions that relate to where they are. Even if they are not sure where the scene is leading, they should do everything with 100 per cent confidence. Be like a swan: on the surface it is seen to be gliding elegantly along the water, but what the onlooker doesn't see is the kicking underneath that makes this happen.

An improviser is not expected to be especially good at mime – people are not expecting them to be Marcel Marceau or even mime trained, they are there to see an improv show; but those improvisers who have mastered some basic techniques can use this skill to help build the world they are creating.

People can use their powers of observation in practical and easy ways to add some simple actions that will add this colour. It is not unusual for two improvisers to start a scene and just keep to the dialogue, and of course there is nothing wrong with this. However, the lack of activity can make the actors self-conscious if they are struggling to find what to say, particularly if they are relying only on dialogue to drive the scene forwards. This can potentially make the whole scene 'sticky', and causes the actors to panic, and to draw on exaggerated offers to try and save it.

Improv stages are regularly quite small, but this doesn't mean that we need to stand in one spot or not be dynamic. We can use simple stage tricks to make movement on the stage to give the impression that we are anywhere.

IN PRACTICE

When entering a scene, the leading actor is expected to, and usually does, have the germ of an idea of where to start. Who becomes the leading actor is usually established because they are the first to rush to the stage with enthusiasm: this tends to be a signal to their troupe that they have something to start with. Some beginners can take a while to appreciate this – that the opening offer does not necessarily have to be verbal. It can also be physical, or both simultaneously.

When a scene is started, anything is there for the taking. The audience is looking at a blank, empty stage, so it is the actor's job to fire their

A big physical can be a fun way to open a scene, even if you are not sure where the scene will go next – someone from your team can join in to help figure it out.

imaginations and fill it with the world we want them to see.

The amazing thing about mime theatre is that if you, as an actor, show the audience something with conviction, then it appears in their mind's eye, and you need to maintain that illusion consistently so that it doesn't disappear.

As to the 'who, what, where' of a scene, using space work is the actor's opportunity to embellish each of these: the 'where' by what you are doing (if you consider the 'where' to involve an activity – imagine you are golfing); the 'who' by how you are doing it (is one of you a caddie?); while the 'what' usually falls into place from these.

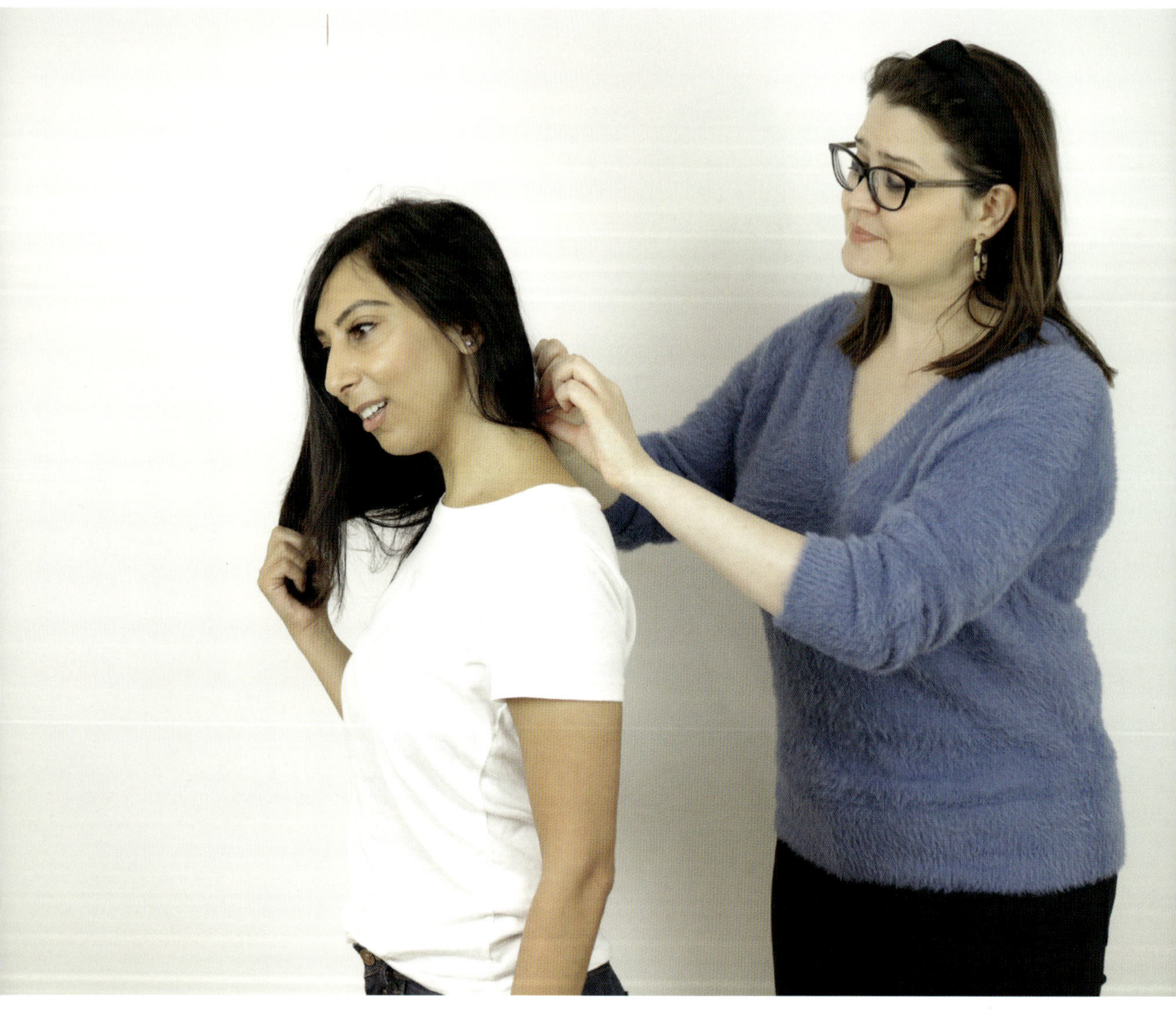

The improvisers are using an imaginary object to help build the relationship between their characters. The object itself can have significance as to who they are to each other.

Take your time, show them things relevant to where you are. If you are in a garden, smell the flowers, hear the insects, take in the fresh air. This will settle both you and the audience, and your scene partners.

If you are in a kitchen, do something – make tea if you are really stuck, and while doing it, model the space on you own kitchen. Where do you keep everything? Kettle, teabags, milk, sugar – open the fridge door and take things out, use them, then put them back and close the door. Keep it all consistent. By doing this, especially at the top of the scene, you are building this world for the audience to see, as you then step into your dialogue.

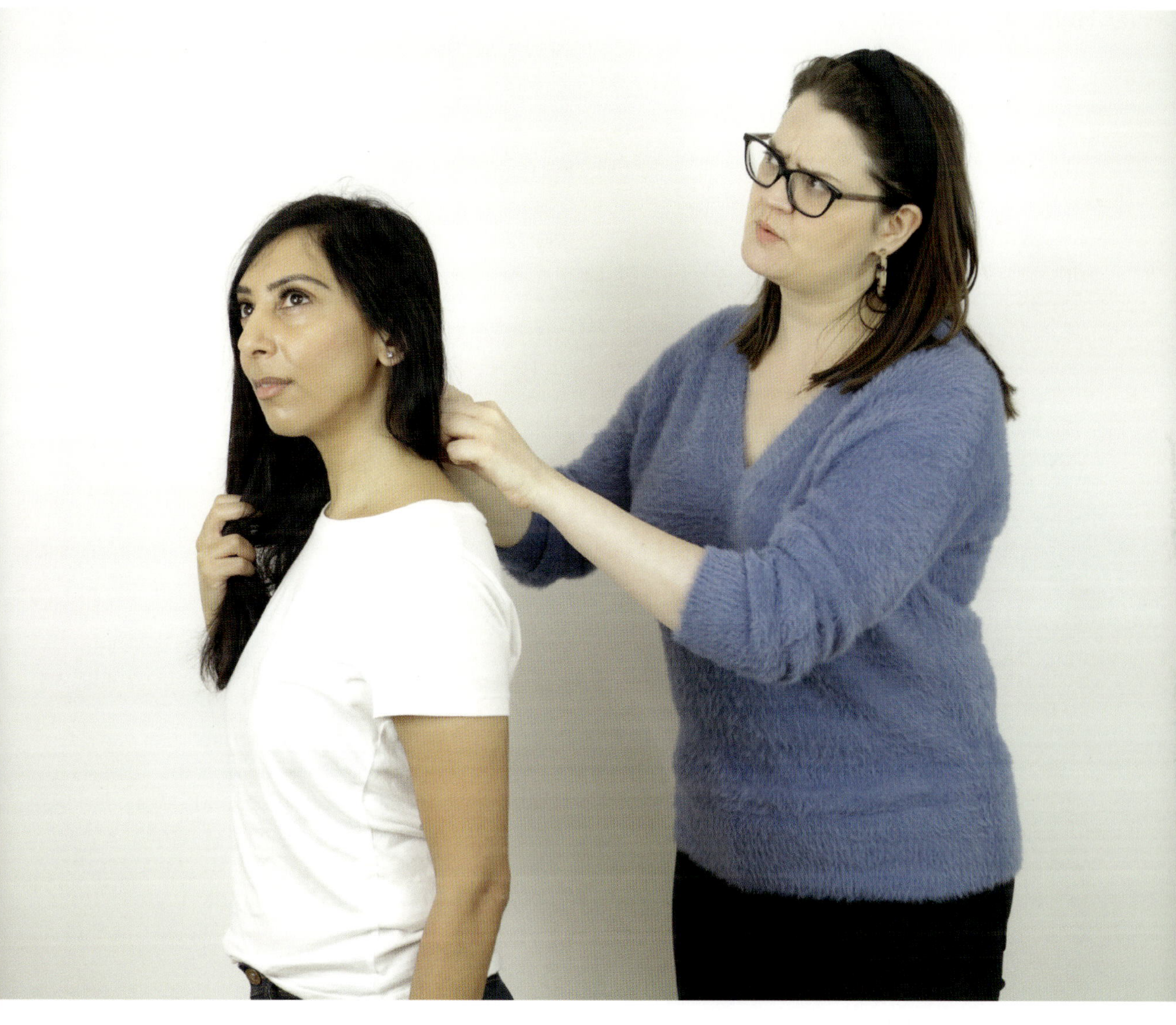

The scene may start with a physical offer, and it may take a few lines for the improvisers to figure out the relationship. This is why it is important to keep applying 'Yes, and…' to each offer as it occurs.

Apart from putting the audience at ease, this strategy also gives them the impression that the actors know what they are doing – which we don't really because we are improvising. The building of this world also helps the actor, as now they can find something to do while they work in their head to figure out what it is they are to say next in order to drive the scene.

Silence is also acceptable if the audience is aware and certain of where you are: building the world for them to see does this. In a scene where two people are fishing, there would be nothing unusual about the characters being silent for a time, and the conversation being relaxed. So why would an improvised scene be any different to that?

Building a World

- Make it clear where you are (this can also be helped verbally).
- Find something to do – anything!
- What tools would you find there?
- Use your senses, too: comment on the smells, views or feeling of a place.
- Be consistent: if you put your glass of wine down on an imaginary table, remember where it is. Audiences are smart, they will remember, so if you stay consistent, they will believe you more.
- Wherever you are, and no matter what type of character you are playing, you are an expert – this means that if you are flying an aeroplane, you should play it as a competent character. This will give you time as an actor to think about what to say.

Let's say the location offered to the actors is a garage. One actor might make the choice that it is a commercial mechanical garage, where vehicles are being serviced. What kind of character would this be? How would they look and act, and what might they be doing right now on a normal day?

In this example you make the choice that you are working on a car repair, so a good start would be to have your head under the bonnet and a tool in one hand. Even if as an actor you know nothing about car engines, you should give the impression that you do: it is important that you always play the character as being competent, unless incompetency is endowed on you, or is part of a game.

When the scene starts, you may be tempted to begin to speak about the task you are carrying out, and this is all right at the top of the scene – though remember not to make the scene about this, but move on to the relationship between you and your scene partner.

When you come out from under the car bonnet, remember it is there. This may seem small and trivial, but the audience will see it, and notice if you stand straight up 'through' it, or duck so as to 'weave' your head out from under it. This can be

happening while you engage in dialogue with your scene partner.

Moreover, don't forget you have a tool in your hand: this can't evaporate, and you need to do something with it. Where is your toolbox? Put it away, maybe take something else out and continue to work on the car as you add more dialogue. You can then add to this by removing the bonnet stand and allowing the bonnet to drop gently. Remember with older cars you need to lean gently on the closed bonnet for it to click closed.

These few simple mimed actions will give the audience the feeling that they are looking through the fourth wall at a scene happening in a garage, and they are more likely to stay engaged. Remember to stay with it: what else could be around you?

Here you have led with a physical offer of working on a car. Immediately this gives the other actor an opportunity to 'Yes, and…' this offer by being either a customer or a colleague. The creation of this world does not have to stop there, as the actors can continue to add objects one might find in a garage. Other vehicles can be added to the stage (if room), cups of tea, tools.

This example came to mind because I once ran a class where the scene was in a commercial car repair shop. We were focusing on space work, and the students were asked to really go for the detail of the activity they were doing. The scene began with one actor, the mechanic, closing a bonnet, and as he lowered it, he struggled with its weight. The other actor, playing the customer, helped to take some of the weight and so they lowered and closed it.

The actor playing the customer commented on the fact that the mechanic was having problems with his left arm again. In the scene it transpired that the mechanic had broken this arm many years before in a car accident involving both characters. The accident was caused by the customer, and he is now married to the mechanic's ex-high-school sweetheart. This history is known to the characters, but they get on with things as normal because they are old

MIME IN POPULAR THEATRE

Stones in His Pockets by Marie Jones (1996)

In this two-hander play the two actors perform all the fifteen characters, moving quickly between each of them; they even at times have dialogue between two or more of the characters that one of the actors is playing. *Stones in His Pockets* gives us a great example of how simple and consistent space work can be used to draw the audience in and create a believable world.

As the play starts the audience meet the two main protagonists and are quickly taken into the magic of character switching, and the use of simple and basic mime skills. The magic here, and where it meets improvisation, is the blank empty stage and the use of minimum props. Props include a few hats, a trunk and a couple of small stools.

Over the course of the play we see the actors mime drinks, food, animals, a variety of objects, and even handshakes and interactions with other characters (who are visibly not there, as the same actor is playing both). The secret here, aside from the skill and talent of the actors, is the consistency the actors maintain. They never let a mimed prop evaporate or forget where it is.

Our Town by Thornton Wilder 1938

Our Town was devised for performance with as few props and as little stage design as possible, and the actors mime the objects, including the milkman's horse and cart, which appears in every act. This play was performed in 2007 at the Mill Theatre in Dublin, with Arclite Productions, and in this production the director used sound effects when necessary to support the use of props.

school friends and now as middle-aged men live in the same neighbourhood.

The beauty of this scene was that the offer came from the *mimed* detail of the weight of the car bonnet, which led to the story of the arm, and so on. Without that offer, and the actor playing the customer picking up on it, we may not have got this lovely history-rich robust story of these characters.

Hypothetically it could be argued that more time would have been spent talking about what was wrong with the car, and what needed to be fixed.

USING OBJECTS

To become an expert on using objects in mime, an actor needs to take mime classes. A very comprehensive practical mime instruction book is *Mime the Gap* (2018), by Richard Knight.

Beginners, and even some experienced players, will often pick up an object, or they are handed one, but after a few seconds it 'evaporates' into the air because they forget to 'do' anything with it. When working on an empty stage it is useful to imagine the location of a coffee table, or a kitchen table or an office desk (whichever the scene may require) – for example at centre stage right on the fourth wall, at the top of the stage. This helps to remind you to 'put down' an object, if necessary.

To get used to how objects feel and interact with your body takes some daily observations. For example, in your day-to-day life, pick up a cup containing a hot drink and observe how it feels. How do you hold your hands around it? How do you (carefully) sip it, and how does it make you feel – do you make any vocal reaction, or any facial expressions? Make a mental note of how you experience this in real life. Put it down and pick it up again. How does it weigh? How does it change the tension in your hand and arm, in your whole body?

Do the same for any other object you interact with: driving a car, using a shovel, playing chess – whatever it is, a time will come when you will

Using objects that may be normal within the environment, the characters really draw in the audience; this helps the actors, as they are less concerned with having to speak, because they are still acting even by doing the action.

need to mime these actions in an improvised scene, so take time to observe, and be aware of how you behave in these situations. Write down your observations and look at them before your next improv class. Use them in a scene and enjoy them – and don't think that you are slowing the story down, because it's the detail that the people watching love. When you get the opportunity in a scene, try using you muscle memory to recreate how the object felt in real life. And remember to be consistent!

MAKING PHYICAL OFFERS

It is a common misconception that a scene needs to be led by a verbal offer. This comes from the fact that most scenes are led by dialogue – but this

AN EXAMPLE OF SPACE WORK

A good example of simple and consistent space work in a scene was performed by a student playing a scuba diver in the classroom during his training. He was performing with another student. This actor took control of the verbal part of the scene, and kept talking about all the amazing things they were going to see once they got into the water. The first actor gave very little in terms of adding to the scene with dialogue, but instead focused all his attention on putting on his diving gear. Obviously this was something he had done in real life.

This actor began by adjusting his tank, and making sure it was at the right pressure (this dialogue he shared with his scene partner). He then gently placed it aside, and pulled out his wetsuit. He spent several moments struggling his feet through its legs, and pulling it up round his waist – adding a small joke about rearranging himself to be comfortable in it, which evoked a giggle from those watching. He then pushed his arms carefully through the suit, rubbing the suit arms as he did so to expel the air (as would be done in a real-life situation). He picked up his mask, but before placing it over his face he turned his back to his scene partner and said, 'Could you zip me up, please?'

His scene partner obliged, to which he replied 'Thanks, you still need to get ready, so I'll see you down there.' He closed the scene by putting on his diving tank and mask, then simulated falling back into the water, to a joyous response from the people watching.

The feedback with this example was that there are times when very little needs to be said to create a character.

HOW SPACE WORK CAN HOLD A SCENE

I recall a *Livewired* show where the suggestion from the audience was 'blade'. My scene partner ran on and began space work, which looked as if she were cutting paper with a paper guillotine. To be honest, I wasn't sure what was happening, so I decided to mirror the offer, which meant both of us were doing the same action on the stage. Unknown to me, my scene partner had no more to offer other than this action, which left us on stage for several seconds without dialogue (in reality it felt like forever). Eventually my scene partner turned to me and said 'Long day, huh?' – to which I nodded in an exasperated fashion, the crowd erupted in laughter, and the MC called the scene.

In retrospect, the learning curve here was again that consistent space work and a calm presence on stage, with good editing to call the scene, can be engaging for the audience. Luckily this was a multi-scene format, so our characters were able to return and give more information as to why the first scene had no dialogue, and what we were doing. Nevertheless it was still a funny experience, and an example of how space work can hold a scene.

doesn't always have to be the case. A physical offer at the top of the scene can be great fun to play with, and the 'Yes, and…' to this sort of offer can be split into two options: mirror the offer, or add to it.

Mirror the offer: Your scene partner is performing a physical action and has not yet given any dialogue. You are not sure what it is they are doing as it is not obvious, so you mirror it by copying them.

- It can happen that the offering actor is carrying out a move, but has no idea of what it is, and is waiting for his scene partner to help him out. This is not as scary as it sounds, and it can be great fun getting in and out of this kind of trouble.
- The best way to deal with this is to get on with the 'who, what, where' and then justify the action you are performing (see 'Freeze tag' as an exercise to help you in this type of situation).

ABOVE: The improvisers are folding a blanket or sheet, and this action would give plenty of options as to who they might be to each other, and where they are. They could be in a park, a laundry room, a hotel room – there are many options.

The improvisers are working together in a very symmetrical way by mirroring each other.

They continue the mime work to confirm to the audience exactly what they are doing; if they allow the blanket to disappear and revert back to dialogue, the audience would be disappointed.

BELOW: The mime at this point needs to be seen through to the end of the folding of the blanket, as the improvisers have already committed to it.

When the improvisers complete the folding task they have committed to as part of the scene, one character takes it over; the dialogue will continue throughout.

Add to the offer: Your scene partner is giving a physical offer that you recognize, so you are able to give the appropriate 'Yes, and…' offer to it. The offer could be chopping wood or washing dishes. The addition can be piling the chopped wood or drying the dishes. Now think about who would be doing this activity together?

- Chopping wood? Two farmers or people preparing for the winter? What could their relationship be? Why are they there? There are plenty of open questions you could address to open the scene with dialogue.
- Washing dishes? This might involve a couple, flatmates, students, workers in a commercial kitchen. Again, there are plenty of options to

choose from, and the same open questions could apply in response to the 'who, what, why'.

The offer could be recognizable, but it may make sense to copy it anyway. For example, fishing.

WHY CONSISTENCY IS IMPORTANT

There needs to be consistency in a scene for the audience to believe an object is there. If it 'disappears' as the actors get into their dialogue, then it weakens the scene. For example, one character hands the other a mug of coffee. The character holding the coffee then begins to make hand gestures that in real life would spill or drop the coffee – but as soon as they have finished their monologue the coffee is obviously back in their hand. So this is inconsistent: first the actor is holding the mug of coffee, then it appears that he isn't, then apparently he is – and the audience sees this, and something even as small as a mug of coffee 'disappearing' and then 'reappearing' can break the illusion that the actors have worked so hard to create.

The exception to this is if the object is 'endowed' on them by the other actors through dialogue; for example: 'I see, Pirate Jones, that you are holding your sword', when the actor playing Pirate Jones now has no choice but to carry a sword. Generally the audience doesn't mind this type of inconsistency – at the start of the scene Pirate Jones didn't appear to be carrying a sword, and apparently now he is – as they know that the object has been endowed on him in real time – and the reaction of the endowed actor would generally induce a laugh. At the top of a scene the audience allows this, but as the scene settles, it is better that actors avoid doing this.

Space work tends to be the last of the skills that improvisers work on in training, or even when they are performing. This can lead to scenes with talking heads and no activity.

How Does it Work with Characters?

The use of space work is a great way to set up an activity or a world, yet at the same time the actor should try to avoid just talking about what they are doing. The dialogue should be of a different topic. Think about when you are doing an activity with a friend. You don't just talk about the activity! It may be part of the conversation to open, but it would not be the central subject of what you talk about. For example, say you are preparing dinner for your partner or friend: they are there with you in the kitchen, and usually you would chat about how the day went, or what recent crisis either of you might have had in your life.

The activity or world you've built is a great way to get a quick impression of what your character may be feeling at that time, as it helps establish why they are doing this, and who they are with. An example could be that the character is in a frenzy cooking, and rushing around the kitchen to make sure everything is ready to serve at the same time. This could be an offer to the scene partner, who may open with a statement such as: 'You seem

---

MOVEMENT AND SPACE WORK

In the most popular television shows or films, the characters are doing something most of the time, even if it is drinking tea or smoking a cigarette. The Brad Pitt character in the 'Ocean' series of films is always eating, but in an interview Brad Pitt the actor explained that the reason for this behaviour was that the character Rusty was always on the move and constantly busy so never had time to sit down for a meal. Brad Pitt's character in *Moneyball* had a similar habit, which was taken directly from the real-life person he was playing.

This is an example of movement and space work that improvisers can take into their scenes. We will look more closely at characters in Chapter 6, Making the Audience Care.

anxious, your workload is still overwhelming you, then!' And the reply to this could be simple: 'Yes, the property business is booming right now and we are working hard to stay ahead of the competition.' This example is dialogue that was inspired by the activity of the person doing the space work.

PLAYING ANIMALS AND INANIMATE OBJECTS

Playing animals and inanimate objects can be great fun, and adds plenty of colour to a scene. It may be done by the extras off-stage jumping in as a dog or a cat, or as a wild animal, if for example the scene is set in a wildlife or national park. The extras do not necessarily add dialogue or interfere with the scene, they are just there to help the actors on stage.

Animals can also be played as the centrepiece of the scene, such as, for example, a couple of male penguins waiting for their wives to return home from hunting, or anything that takes your fancy. A way to prepare for this is to watch nature programmes and observe how animals move and interact with each other. If they were speaking, what might they be saying (if they had our level of communication)? These can make interesting scenes, as we don't get an everyday insight into such things. For example, a scene with two cats chatting about their owners could be fun. Think of it as a cartoon where animals are the stars.

In the cat example, the essence of the space work would be the calm and settled nature of a mature cat. Remaining very still, maybe taking a moment to groom itself, its demeanour can be easily mimicked, which could be very effective in

A group of improvisers playing marine life. They could be in a household tank or in the wild – this would be up to the improvisers, and which verbal offer they led with.

The stage position shows that the improvisers facing out are the protagonists in this scene, while the improviser crossing as a different type of marine life is adding some texture to the scene without interfering.

drawing the people watching into this world. Any well known cat personality traits might also be included, such as curiosity, grace, intuitiveness and territorial behaviour. These factors can be demonstrated through dialogue and with facial expressions. Add other social factors to these, such as the status between the cats, and you really begin to fill in the world.

There is no need to over-complicate things, or try to force a complex interesting story: just play it for real. A previous improv teacher told me once when I was playing a chicken: 'If you are a chicken, just be a chicken!' From an audience point of view, getting an insight into what two domestic cats might be saying to each other is fun and engaging. From an improviser's point of view, this type of acting can be great fun to play.

Inanimate objects are also a great way to add colour to a scene. These should be things that would be seen in that particular world: for example if the scene is set in a woodland or forest area, you could jump in and be a tree. Be careful with this, though: you will be in the same position for some time, and it will get tiring to stay still with your arms held out as a tree.

As with animals, inanimate objects can also be the stars of a scene. On this theme there is a very funny comedy sketch from Michael McIntyre about various spices in a kitchen cupboard, where they are all complaining about how little they get used, and are wondering what is so special about salt and pepper. A variation on this that I have seen was of a bowl of fruit where the actors personified the different fruits, with some having dreams of one

An improviser playing a household pet; exactly what may be made obvious by the dialogue added, or could be defined by the improviser's body shape.

BELOW: The main point of the story is of two cats competing over territory. Animals or inanimate objects are great fun to play, and are also fun to watch.

day being in a fruit salad or fruit juice, while others feared for their lives and were instead planning an escape, with dreams of making it home to South America and becoming a tree and raising a family of fruit of their own.

SUMMARY

Practise with real objects:

- Practise how a real object feels: its weight, tension and shape. Use this muscle memory with imaginary objects when you next do a scene.
- Remember consistency: as you would with real objects, remember where you've put them if you put them down.
- Spend time doing things you wouldn't normally do: if you don't spend much time gardening, then try it out and pay attention to the feel and technique of the tools you use.
- Be an expert at whatever it is you are doing: looking competent gives the audience the impression you know exactly what you are doing, even if in your head you are struggling to think of what to say.
- Animals can join a scene as background.
- Animals can be the stars of the scene.
- Inanimate objects add colour to a scene.

EXERCISES

- If you have a pet, look at how it moves: it can be anything from a dog to a goldfish.
- Spend some time in the natural world: try and get out to the countryside, and if that is not possible, then to a local park.
- Take notice of the wildlife you encounter; ask yourself what might be going on in their mind if they could think as you do.

USING REAL PROPS

In our *Livewired* show we had the luxury of a prop bag containing an assortment of bits and bobs for us to take on stage and use. These props could be used as they were, or as a substitute for something it could be mistaken for. For example, a Russian fur hat was used several times as a small pet.

- If this is not possible, watch nature programmes.
- Try mimicking them and make up your own little stories.
- Watch nature programmes with someone, and play a game where you speak for the animals.
- Meanwhile, a great exercise is where you throw yourselves into a situation based on one word; animals and inanimate objects work really well here, and the scenes are short.
- Meanwhile… (*see* games index).
- Foreign film: (see games index) the players acting can use the opportunity to introduce an object and be really physical.
- Freeze tag is great practice for quickly thinking of why characters are in the position they are in.

EVERYDAY LIFE

- Being happy with silence and getting used to filling a space is a great habit that can help you when standing in front of a crowd.
- Being aware of your body keeps you conscious of good posture.
- Becoming aware of movement, of yourself and of others helps you tune in to reading body language.

4
SPONTANEITY AND LISTENING

There are various techniques and exercises to help actors get out of their head and stay connected to the scene or game and to their fellow improvisers. For many beginners a difficult skill to master is to think on the spot and react to what is happening in front of them. However, there are many improv games that are designed to force people out of their heads and into the moment.

There tend to be two main factors that block spontaneity. First, some of us may hold back from speaking out because we are afraid that what we say will not be a good enough contribution to the conversation or situation – but we feel frustration when someone else says exactly what we were thinking and gets a great reaction to it.

Second is the simple reality that we are not listening, or at least not listening properly. In our heads we may be thinking about what we want to say next, and so we are not 'in the moment'.

Improv as an art form and a hobby is great for addressing both blockers. We learn that being spontaneous is a brave act that can sometimes go wrong, but if you keep with it your aptitude for wit gets stronger and you will start to take more risks. Before you know it, you are the one making the witty contributions to a group conversation. And to make sure you don't miss these opportunities you should stay alert and be aware of your surroundings. Begin to take more heed of what is going on around you.

IN PRACTICE

In improvisation, fight or flight is always present. Flight occurs when we panic and go blank, or we make crazy offers that derail the story; this tends to surface as crude behaviour, inappropriate language or just unnecessary gags to try and save the situation. Fight, on the other hand, composes us: we rely on our training, and reply knowing that even if it goes wrong, the risk is low, and our scene partners are there to help us out.

When we stand on stage, everything changes. We become sharper and our senses heighten. We are paying attention to everything that is going on with the scene and our scene partner. We are watching their facial expressions, body language and movement, and are listening not only to what they are saying, but how they are saying it. What is their tone of voice, what offer can I make in response to 'Yes, and…'? It doesn't always have to be a verbal 'yes', and the more attention we pay to who is on stage with us, the more options we give ourselves.

A state of panic will cause the actor to improvise in an erratic way. The fight or flight concept is important, and trusting your instinct and being in survival fight mode is where we need to be for spontaneity to thrive. The physical demeanour of a lioness when she is stalking her prey and when she is relaxing with her pride is quite different: during the hunt, every movement she makes is calculated and exact, so she does not scare her prey. When the hunt is on, she is ever present.

Having drama in a scene is always interesting to an audience, and we should do our best to make sure we are still applying 'Yes, And…' and not letting the drama or the egos of the improviser take over.

And from the other side, see the prey. We have all seen how a rabbit, for example, is quietly eating its food, then it hears a crackle – and suddenly it's alert, its ears have popped up and it is ready to sprint away.

This is where everything around you becomes clear, and this tends to happen organically, when danger presents itself.

It would not be unusual for an improviser suddenly to explode into an argument between the characters in order to save a floundering scene. If the tension in the scene escalates it quickly steals much of the story from the audience.

Good improvisers can normalize the scene again, so that the escalating tension does not take over.

PRACTISING LISTENING

One of the blockers to listening is that a person is not listening because they are waiting to speak again, and are paying more attention to what they want to say next. This may also be a defence mechanism to protect their point of view or their standpoint on the topic in discussion, and because they won't be changed by the other side of the conversation. We are organic creatures, and being reluctant to change can make a person unable to adapt to the circumstances around them, which in turn can block spontaneity and lead to some anxiety when they are put outside their comfort zone.

To begin this listening journey, have a conversation with someone you are close to in your life with whom you feel safe, and try this exercise. Pick a topic of conversation where you have opposing views – it doesn't have to be something of extreme importance to you, such as political views, it can be more like your favourite

Good eye contact is essential for improvisers to 'tune in' and listen properly to each other.

pasta dish, or your favourite album of a band you both like – and instead of standing firm, and not accepting anything your opponent says, instead listen with an open mind, and see if it changes you. You may find that your conversation style changes, so you challenge points as a way of learning to try and take a different standpoint. You may also see that it enhances your level of empathy.

As actors, we portray people who change over the course of the film or play, and our job is to present that change to the audience over the course of the story. The audience sees the world change through the eyes of the protagonist, and for it to be believable we need to see the character listening and being changed by the environment and those around them.

At the beginning of the class or workshop a couple of exercises on mindfulness and listening can really help people hone their listening skills.

Normalizing a scene can save it from dying – keep calm and composed, and keep listening to your scene partner.

Mindfulness and Improvisation

As a warm-up for any class, rehearsal or show the group should be taken through a few moments of mindfulness to settle everyone into the space. This does not need to be over-indulged – no more than two to three minutes of breathing and becoming aware of one's own body would be sufficient.

This exercise is useful because everyone will have come from different places, and not all will have had a relaxing period to get themselves into the right frame of mind. Some may have come straight from their place of work, or may have rushed out from a busy schedule with a young family. Others could have had a stressful commute.

Taking a few moments at the start of the session gets everyone into the same frame of mind and helps settle those who need it, and makes everyone present relax. The exercise proceeds as follows:

- Get everyone in a circle.
- Ask them to take a relaxed stance with their feet shoulder-width apart.
- Ask them to relax their shoulders so they don't lift on an intake of breath.
- Ask everyone to close their eyes.
- In a gentle tone of voice talk the group through a series of breaths. You don't need to be a yoga expert to do this: it's a simple one-minute exercise to settle people into the room.
- After one minute of slow, steady breathing, ask them to open their eyes.
- Check everyone is all right before moving on.

Names in a circle:

- In the circle ask everyone in turn to call out their first name.
- Make it clear if the rotation is to go clockwise (to your left) or anti-clockwise (to your right).
- Start with yourself.
- After a couple of rounds, switch rotation direction.

Once this naming energy is spinning round the circle at a decent pace, stop the group and adjust the rules:

- Tell them you are going back to the first rotation direction.
- Instead of saying their own name, they should say the name of the person to their immediate right.
- Send it round once and see what happens.

Even though you have spent several minutes with everyone establishing their own name, when it comes to naming the people beside them, this usually causes hesitation. This is because in the first level of the exercise all were preoccupied with getting their own name right. This sounds silly, but it is amazing what a little pressure can do to people's attention and confidence.

This is because the moment we stop listening to what is going on around us, we begin to focus on what is in our heads instead. The group members were repeating their own names in their heads in order to make sure that when their turn came, they didn't make a mistake and look silly.

At this point I always ask the group how many of them would admit that they were in their own heads, even with a task as simple as saying their own first name when their turn arrived. This is a great comfort to the group when they realize that they are not the only ones who were distracted in this exercise, and now that they are aware of it, they have made the first step in staying out of their head and getting into the moment.

Listening Exercise for Beginners

- Split the group into pairs.
- Assign an A and a B to each person.
- Ask A to tell B about their day so far, up to just before the class started: what time they got up; how they travelled to work (did any interesting things happen on that journey?); how the morning went, what they had for lunch, and so on.

After a minute, ask B to tell A what they heard, and what they might have picked up between the lines: such as, on the way to work you were quite happy/sad because when you spoke of it your face lit up/was strained, and this stayed with you all morning until lunch when you met your friend and were cheered up by their good news of a new job – and so on…

The point is not for B to get it right, but to pay more attention to what A is saying, and *how* they are telling their story. A can respond with how close B may have got to how they were feeling at certain points of the day. Then swap the exercise between them.

Not only is this a great exercise for getting people to tap into their listening skills, but it also connects the players with each other, and can be a good exercise for a new group.

Listening Exercise for a Group

- Ask all players to think of a favourite grievance they have (such as cyclists on the footpath, or anything that niggles them but is not essentially disruptive to their life in a broader sense).
- Split the group into pairs.
- Assign an A or a B to each person.
- Ask A to share their grievance with B, and to elaborate why it bothers them.
- After about a minute, ask B to tell us what they really think bothers A about the grievance: is it

something they think bothers them at face value, or is there an underlying issue?
• Swap to B and repeat the exercise.

This exercise can be done with a group of strangers, but people can play it safe with their interpretations, so it works better with a group of people who know and trust each other.

When we are not present, we are stuck in our heads, dwelling on what it is we may say next, and overthinking any response we are cultivating. We do this to stay safe – safe from ridicule that what we say next will not be accepted. Think about it as fight or flight: we are most in the moment when something is at stake; when times are quiet, we don't need to be so alert.

THE IMPORTANCE OF SPONTANEITY

In a rehearsal once, we were playing a tagging game where one person is on a date, and the other person is played by three actors, each of whom has a different state of mind: nervous, loving and chivalrous (myself).

The date took place in a wooded area. The actor playing 'nervous' spotted a squirrel and began to act nervously, so my instinct as 'chivalrous' was to tag in and defend my date from this menacing squirrel. So I gave the line, '*Back*, Squirrel – I will defend you, young maiden!' Now this brought a lot of laughter to the rehearsal, as it was the spontaneity that made it funny.

Almost exactly the same situation presented itself in a show not long after, and I repeated the gag – but this time it didn't work. After the show I spoke with my artistic director about it, as he had been there when the same thing happened in rehearsal, and he told me that the reason it hadn't worked this time was because it wasn't spontaneous. And he's right: in improvised comedy, you can't beat spontaneity. Rehearsed gags don't work, they look stale, and the genuinely 'of the moment' quality isn't there – and the audience can sense this.

AWARENESS

A great side effect of practising awareness is that you will begin to tune in to the world around you, and to take heed of the people in your life. What are they saying, and how are they saying it? Try and be aware of how they might be feeling. What is their body language telling you, and their tone of voice?

Who are these people who always seem to have a witty comment to make? They are usually perceived as being smart, intelligent, because they know the right thing to say at the right time. But this is because they are present and in the moment, and they have got to this point by practising it.

'Practising' doesn't mean spending time working on being aware – to some this comes naturally. It could even be a trait inherited from a parent, and a person may not know that they are behaving in this way, as each of us has a different sense of awareness. It starts with listening, and listening properly:

• To become more aware of yourself and what is happening around you, start with how you breathe. Make this the centrepoint of your thoughts. If your mind wanders, just come back to breathing.
• Pay more attention to what is going on around you: next time you go to the shop, try and take in some details – how many people you passed, what buses or other things of interest you saw.
• When having a conversation, pay more attention to what the person is saying to you. Is there anything else you are picking up from that person?

Listening – or to listen *actively*, as it is widely known – does take some practice. And to begin with you are listening as an improviser, which means that making mistakes is allowed; as you improve on this skill you can then take it into your personal and professional life, but for now try to focus on listening as an improviser. When improvising you are in a situation where risk is low, and your 'Yes, and…' is always valid.

Increasing Your Awareness

In improv you can increase your awareness when listening in the following ways:

- Pay attention to how the other actor delivers the line: are they glad, sad, mad or in fear? What sub-feeling of these do you get from them: are they ecstatic maybe, or just content, maybe suspicious or jealous? Whatever it is, try and take note of it, as this can be used in your response.
- What are they trying to tell you? Listen for information you can add to.
- Give them space to finish their thought.
- Now you have taken note, you can respond with your 'Yes, and…'

This is where people get scared, thinking what if my response is boring or over the top? The best thing to do here is to trust your instinct. If you get it wrong, it doesn't matter, your scene partner will support you. We worry too much about making mistakes in front of others, and so we keep our reactive thoughts to ourselves. Therefore, using the opportunity as an improviser is a great way to practise in a low-risk environment.

The more mistakes you make, the more resilient you become at getting feedback. You will find a way to take it on the chin with humour. If this becomes second nature to you, you become braver and think less of what you say (get yourself into trouble and sort it out). Mistakes are a gift: true improvisers never see them as a mistake, they see them as opportunities or gifts, and use them to their best advantage.

THE DARK SIDE OF IMPROV

The improvisation art form has many techniques that bring about a positive frame of mind and acceptance of your scene partner. We have looked at the many ways we can make scenes and games work, but there are times when people purposely ignore these collaborative rules and make life difficult for their partner. This can happen with many people at different levels of experience. See overleaf for some common examples of what frustrates players when they find themselves in scenes where the interaction has been described as toxic.

Be Nice

Bear in mind that people may be turning up in a state of mind that could be driving their behaviour. Be nice, remember you are on the same team, and at the end of the day we all want our improvised stories, games and scenes to work. If you are patient and respectful, you will gain the other's trust, and in time you will see these bad habits dissolve.

HITTING A PLATEAU

The other dark side to improv is when an improviser has reached their current peak and is on top form, but then at some point they feel that their ability begins to drop. This happens from time to time with most people in many disciplines – musicians and songwriters, sportspeople, actors and writers. This has been described as 'hitting diminishing returns', where there starts to be more frustration than joy in your artistic endeavours. The cause of the plateau could be for several reasons:

- Not improvising for a while and having the feeling of not being match fit.
- Getting to a performance comfort zone and not pushing yourself into a new stretch zone.
- Relying on certain stock characters or situations in your repertoire.
- Feeling as if your creativity is being blocked by another player you frequently play with.
- A genuine lack of interest.

EXAMPLE SITUATIONS

Example Situation One

There are times when you are playing the game and your partner is infuriating to work with. You don't say anything, and you try to save a scene whilst being polite and open-minded to what your scene partner may offer along the way. You find it difficult to 'Yes, and...' to the scene because the early offers are too surreal, and you feel the story is becoming unhinged and you could be losing the audience.

Potential Solution

It can be difficult in the moment, but take a step back and make an attempt at slowing the scene down a little. Think about how you could normalize the scene and characters. An obvious choice would be to make the surreal character have a reason for their behaviour, but this really just calls out the fact that things are weird. Think about how to make this acceptable to the audience:

- Match their level of surrealness: are the characters surreal in a normal world, or are they normal characters in a surreal world?
- Do your best to make the other person look good: an offer to bring the characters together is usually appreciated here.
- You don't have to save the scene, just go with it and make some mental notes to chat with your scene partner about afterwards.

Example Situation Two

Feelings of frustration, or even hidden frustration, are a valid emotion, especially when your scene partner deviates from improv frameworks designed to support the successful creation of characters, scene work and emotions. You are not sure how to deal with such improvisers, and so you avoid doing scenes with them if you can.

Potential Solution

When faced with frustrations in playing with certain people, it is good to take a moment and think about what it is they are doing that is frustrating you. It may not be that they are being difficult, it could be that the frustration is with your own expectations of how you feel the scene should go. So relax with it all and try to apply some basic principles again. Endow them, be strong with it, and be nice. Give them the benefit of the doubt, and continue to be as generous as you can.

If you figure out that the frustration is from the other player playing for the gag and working to make their own funny, there is no harm in having a friendly conversation about it if you feel you have a close enough relationship with them. But be careful if you decide to have this conversation, as you might be scratching the surface of an insecurity.

Example Situation Three

Your scene partner defaults to making gags: their focus is on being funny by taking on characters under the influence of alcohol or drugs, and you feel that they are only trying to make themselves look good. Regardless of the offers you make to normalize things, your partner continues to block you and focuses on a conflict to drive what you feel is cheap comedy or forced drama. Playing a person 'under the influence' allows them to be as uncooperative and aggressive as they want, in what you may feel is a disastrous piece of storytelling that actually has no story, only pointless conflict.

Potential Solution

What is the reason for their behaviour? Is it a default character or situation this player goes to? As you would in real life, give them the benefit of the doubt and hear them out. 'Yes, and...' as best you can, and if you feel the scene has no truth, find a way to end it.

Playing with the same group of improvisers could have this effect, but there are ways to get around this:

- Play with more experienced players than yourself. This may seem daunting, but persevere and you will get to a better level.

- Revisit older groups and see how you and they have changed.
- Beginners are happy and eager to have more experienced players play with them, so do this.
- Mixing the experience level of the players you play with shows you how far you have come since starting, and what gaps you need to fill to move to the next level. Having this mix gives you confidence and motivation.

This is normal, but it is never really talked about. The key is always to have chemistry and rapport with your performing group. It's also worthwhile knowing that with improv, no matter how much experience you have, you need to learn, refresh and grow continuously. One show might not be your show, but the next show may be yours, and the following one will be someone else's. This is what makes improv so special.

SUMMARY

- When in a conversation with someone, as they are speaking, think what the next word might be. Follow the conversation as they are speaking it, and this will clue you in to their frame of mind.
- Stay alert to what you believe is the message you are hearing, and challenge it with a response you think the other person is waiting for.
- Trust your instinct.
- Spontaneity requires a great deal of focus, but this gets easier over time.
- In improvised comedy, spontaneity is gold. Rehearsed gags will not work as well.

EXERCISES

- One-word story: try this exercise with friends, or even as an ice breaker at work as it's a great way

to introduce the concept to people of letting go of control and being in the moment.
- Ask people to trust and watch out for each other: one thing about being spontaneous is that we think we are on our own with our thoughts, but the truth is that people you know who are good at begin spontaneous are usually confident at it, as they have been doing it for a long time. This means that they are confident with speaking out and adding. Learn from that and join in, and treat mistakes as a good thing.
- Play games with your group that are heavy in focus, and soon people will tune in. Bipity-Bopity-Boo is a great exercise for intense focus. Other games might include a game where if they don't listen correctly, they pay a fine (20p for example); whispering games; one-word games (tell a story one word at a time). These games make the players pay attention to what has been said before them. If people hesitate or overthink at any point, call it out. Encourage people to trust their instincts and *say it*!
- 'Meanwhile' (*see* Games Index): this is great for rushing in and thinking on your feet.
- 'Lines from a hat' (*see* Games Index): justify your paper, be quick and spontaneous.

EVERYDAY LIFE

- Make it a game to listen and be spontaneous with your friends or partner, and see what fun it brings up.
- When listening to someone speak of something in their life, see if you can read between the lines.
- Be brave and speak your thought when it comes to you, don't hold it back.
- The more you practise, the better you will get at it.
- Have fun with it: you will soon figure out your own personal comedy style, but you must be brave to find it.

5
FINDING THE GAME

Finding the game is a concept where both actors work to identify the *funny* in the scene, and work together to build a pattern or *game* that will continue to play and escalate. It is a very popular technique in sitcom writing, and also in long-form improvisation.

So what does it mean to find the game of the scene, and to listen to your fellow improvisers and 'make them look good'? Listening correctly gives improvisers a more sincere insight into what is being said, which can lead to picking up and exploring more interesting offers.

TIPS IN FINDING THE GAME

In almost every popular sitcom the process of finding the game is written in. For example, something small happens to a character and escalates slowly. After reading this chapter revisit some of your favourite sitcoms and see if you can spot the game.

As in any game of sport there are rules that the players must observe in order for playing to be possible, and improvisation is no different. We place a structure around us to get a scene up and running – the same applies to an improvised game.

The game of a scene can be understood in more than one way. In short form, the game or the rules/format of the game are predefined, and the players are aware of this before the game starts. The origin of the game could have been determined by a player/director in the past, or it could have happened accidentally in a show or rehearsal, and then evolved into its own format.

The other way to understand the 'game of a scene' is one that is not predefined before the players begin. Instead it happens organically as the players figure out the *funny*. This is usually done by identifying a pattern or a fun escalation of an incident.

Many long-form teachers advise their students to watch popular sitcoms, where the game is a big part of the show. This is very good advice, and if you ask your teacher, they will be able to give you many examples of where this is happening in a sitcom situation.

IN PRACTICE

When a scene starts, anything is possible, depending on the format of the show or scene and the current attitude of the players. A few options are present: firstly, the players may decide to run with a plot or character-based storyline. In this case the scene may be more dramatic and truer to life, where the funny comes from the situation they are in. The game will then arise by the players finding a pattern that will escalate as the scene moves forwards.

Building on the Funny

The scene starts and the players establish the 'who, what, where' to get the scene started and

Finding the game is a fun part of improvising a scene, and it is important for new improvisers to enjoy this part of the art form. It builds great rapport between players.

An improviser enters with a physical offer and tells us who they are.

Another improviser enters and adds to the first offer.

A third improviser enters and adds to the current offer from the actors on stage; this combination of three confirms the game on offer. The scene can continue escalating the game, or using the set-up to run a fun plot based on the game.

settled. At some point early in the scene, one of the players will make an offer that the other finds interesting, and they will reply to the offer either by spinning it from a different angle or enhancing it incrementally. For example, if the scene were zookeepers feeding the animals, it starts with a usual day at the zoo with one keeper saying to the other:

Actor 1: 'I'm concerned for Big Charlie, our silverback. He seems to be losing interest in his food, and he's lost a bit of weight!'

Actor 2: 'Yes, I've seen that too. We should keep an eye on him!'

Enter Actor 3 as Big Charlie; he is dismissive of his food.

Actor 1: 'Yes, you're right, look how melancholy he is!' (This is an offer to Actor 3 playing Charlie to portray a melancholy expression on his face.)

Actor 2: 'You'd swear he was in love by the expression on his face!' (Actor 3 may or may not respond to this offer, and it could become the game of changing faces)

Enter Actor 4 and tags out Actors 1 and 2 (the zookeepers); he takes up position with Actor 3 and begins to play another gorilla.

Actor 4: 'How is the diet going, Charlie? You're looking good!'

Actor 3: 'Not bad, but it's tough going! Those two keep turning up with stems, bamboo shoots and lovely fresh fruit. Tempts me every day!'

Actor 4: 'Stick with it, Charlie, I'm sure if you do, Nancy will go on a date with you to the west side of the enclosure for sunset!'

Actor 3: 'Oh, I hope so, I really like her.'

So now there is a 'funny' opportunity picked up by Actor 4, who introduced the diet story for Big Charlie. Now a possible game here is for each pair of teams to add more things to Big Charlie's appearance: have you noticed Charlie has become more groomed, have you noticed Charlie has become more muscular, and so on…

More extras can get involved and keep escalating Charlie's make-over story. Take him to the barber, the dentist or to the gym, get him fitted for a suit, all the time treating it like a perfectly normal situation.

The concept of the game is to find an opportunity and build on it, taking the audience from a normal day at feeding time at the zoo, and escalating all the way to Big Charlie's big date.

GROUNDED CHARACTERS

The technical term originally for a grounded character is 'straight man', yet women can play this role too, and may be referred to as a 'comic foil'. This makes the term 'straight man' non-inclusive. Also, using the word 'straight' in the description of the character may have a sexual orientation connotation, so I prefer to refer to this type of character as a 'grounded' character.

An example that is quite common is to have one person playing what is generally known as the straight (man) character, or I prefer to call it the person grounded in the real world. Their normality makes the absurdity of the others believable.

A common character in many sitcoms, their job is really to give the comic character lines to pull

TIPS ON BUILDING THE FUNNY

- Start in a mundane fashion: this is an important step in drawing the audience in ('who, what, where').
- Extras joining can be helpful to highlight one aspect of the scene so far (if you are an extra, try not to force it).
- Tag in to isolate the funny item or character in the scene.
- Escalate slowly, otherwise you lose the fun and bring the game to an end too soon.

One character can remain grounded in reality if the other characters are whacky or surreal; this is a great comedy device commonly used.

Alternatively, both characters feel the same way about the same things.

laughs from. An example of this is Sybil Fawlty and Polly in *Fawlty Towers,* and many of the guests. Their normality takes the audience into a realistic place and allows the frantic nature of Basil to be tolerated. If every one of the characters were running at the same speed and intensity and causing the same havoc, we would have difficulty in keeping up – plus the lack of juxtaposed characters would take the fun away.

In the *Fawlty Towers* example, Sybil plays a type of nemesis to Basil, while Polly plays his confidante. These play well into the farcical character of Basil. We find the fun in the constantly disastrous situations that Basil finds himself in.

Another well-known example is the role of Michael Bluth, played by Jason Bateman in the sitcom *Arrested Development*. In this show the fun is turned from what we see in *Fawlty Towers*. Here Michael is the protagonist and so spends his time reacting to and normalizing the whacky characters around him, who are his dysfunctional family.

Having a grounded character in a scene is a great way to find a game. Figuring out who the protagonist is will become obvious once the funny is called out by one of the actors, and so you can decide to play it as a farcical character in the real normal world, or as a grounded character in a surreal world with whacky characters around them.

Using a stock character like this is not always necessary. The game can also be found with all grounded characters and even all surreal characters.

An interesting exception to these is the example of the gorilla sequence related above. In this case the audience is looking at a completely surreal world, where you have a gorilla that can speak and interact with the real world, and has the nature to be in love and spends time preparing for his big date. All the while the characters in the real world pay no heed to the fact that a gorilla is interacting with them, and the audience gets no explanation

It is acceptable for all improvisers to play grounded characters, and the game can be played in a different fashion; in this example the characters are preparing themselves for a night out or an event, and the game could be the synergy between the characters.

As they continue to prepare themselves, they stay aligned and do everything together.

as to why this is possible. In the same way we see the character of Brian the dog in *Family Guy* by Seth MacFarlane. Here the audience can be considered as being grounded, as we are willing to accept this without question and just enjoy the story.

Grounded and Surreal Characters

Grounded and 'whacky' characters can be played in a fashion where one character makes life difficult for the other. The best example that comes to mind is the 'Four Candles/Fork Handles' sketch played by The Two Ronnies, in which Ronnie Barker's character makes life difficult for Ronnie Corbett. It is the increasing frustration of the shopkeeper and the blasé attitude of the customer that makes us laugh.

TIPS ON GROUNDED CHARACTERS

- Decide as quickly as possible who the protagonist is (the audience tend to take the side of the protagonists and can identify with the choices they make).
- Is the character grounded in a surreal world, or are they a farcical character in a grounded world?
- Grounded characters should not get involved in the madness: rather, they should react to it as a normal person would.
- The grounded character's job where the protagonist is farcical is to feed them lines and mundane situations in which they can be funny and absurd.
- The grounded character should be acted sincerely, and the scene usually works best if they are humble in character.

When improvising, the decision of which actor takes which role needs to happen organically. An example is a scene between a father and son, where the father is instilling in his son the traditions of their ancestors; this in itself becomes part of the game, where the father would repeatedly say to the son character: 'As my father taught me when I was your age, and his father when *he* was your age, and his father before him, when *he* was your age.' This dialogue can be repeated as much as the audience allow; once you sense they have had enough of the joke, drop it for the time being – you can always bring it back later in the scene.

The origin of this scene was the father and son on a camping trip, lighting a fire and toasting marshmallows; this escalated into them fishing, then driving, smoking a cigarette and taking drugs, until eventually the son is taken into the family drug-dealing business. So the interest lies in the fact that in the first two scenes the father/son relationship seems normal, but it escalates into something more sinister. This would be an unexpected development for the audience, and so they would enjoy the incremental journey you take them on. This needs practice, and may be led by one of the actors, but ideally using 'Yes, and…' the two actors would share the storytelling.

FINDING THE GAME IN THE PLOT

In the case of a plot or character-based scene, the game is usually secondary or may be found in the relationship between the characters. For example, in a father/son scene, you may have an overbearing father who wants to control the future of his son and have him work in the family business. The son, on the other hand, may have other ambitions, such as to leave home and be an interior designer. The scene in this case may start off with this conversation, and is constantly blocked by the father (this is a good example of when 'no' means 'yes' in the sense of a 'Yes, and…', as discussed in Chapter 2).

The scene could then evolve into a sequence where everything the son does is wrong, or the father disagrees with him, even in a simple task such as making a cup of tea, which would be reached incrementally. The game part of this is setting up a pattern that lulls the audience into a false sense of security, where they think they understand the characters and where the plot is going: this usually brings the laugh at the end of the scene.

In this scene we can see that everything the son does is wrong:

Dad: 'Good job on the deli prep son, looks great and very professional.'
Son: 'I want to go to London to train as an interior designer, Dad.'
Dad: 'An interior designer? You need to stay here and help me with the butcher's shop! Anyway, you wouldn't make a good interior designer, just look at your apartment!'
Son: 'I can learn! Let's talk about it later. I need to go now and make a fresh load of sausages.'
Dad: 'Make sausages? You always forget to add the special ingredient!'
Son: 'I'll remember this time.'
Dad: 'Remember this time? You forget everything, you forgot your phone today – I tried to call you this morning to pick up some special ingredients on your way in!'
Son: 'I left it in my other apron. I'll make tea.'
Dad: 'Good, and while you're there you can serve in the deli.'

It could also work the other way round:

Dad: 'What you up to, son? Taking a break?'
Son: 'Yes Dad, I was just about to start the sausages prep.'
Dad: 'Thanks son, you do a great job on them.'
Son: 'I'd like more responsibility in the shop and factory.'
Dad: 'And you can have it! You are talented!'
Son: 'I'll take on more deliveries.'

Dad: 'You are a great driver, our food always arrives on time!'
Son: 'Yes, I pride myself on that.'
Dad: 'Can you have a look at the factory layout and see what could be made better?'
Son: 'I have some ideas there, such as using less packaging – less is more!'
Dad: 'If you do a good job, I'll pay for you to go to design school and you can be an interior designer, like you talked about when you were a young boy.'
Son: 'Really, Dad?'
Dad: 'Yes, really! Now get back to work, and don't let me catch you slouching around again!'

As with the previous example, the building of the son's future is incremental, and this became the game. The pattern is the consistency of the conversation, always relating to the son's competency.

In the case where the game turns up earlier and happens by accident there is usually less of

a plot around the characters – they are playing with the first funny thing that happens. For this, the player will do their usual work setting up the scene with the 'who, what, where' and establishing the relationship between the characters. Once in place the actors will then start to be aware of what patterns they fall into. Once they do, they can then start to build on it in an incremental fashion.

SPOT THE GAME

How do we know when a game is there? The short answer is practice. The key to finding the game is to listen intensely, and even repeat the line you have just heard in your head. This technique is useful as it can slow the pace of the scene and allow the actors time to process what has been said to them. Doing this makes it easier to find something subtle to react to.

To begin with, it is useful to have a third party there, either a player not in the scene or a director to observe. Their job is to watch the scene and call out when they see an opportunity for a game to begin. They can simply do this with a signal to the players: the most common method is for the observer to call 'game' when they see an opportunity, or you could use a desk bell as a signal.

This works because it is generally easier to see the game emerge when you are not busy playing. For more experienced players you could observe and take notes to share with the players after the scene ends. This is better for people with more experience, because they can start to discover it themselves in real time instead of being prompted.

Either way you will need to spend time playing with your peers and taking chances. Not all attempts will evolve into a successful game, so it is important to practise and even to have many failed attempts.

Another useful exercise is for two players to have a mundane conversation and see what emerges. Allow this to happen for two to three minutes, and afterwards have a discussion with the rest of the group to see who found what interesting, and how it might have escalated.

HEIGHTEN THE GAME

Once you have found the game the next stage is to find a way to heighten it. Start small and build slowly, and be careful not to heighten it too quickly or you will kill the fun. For example, if two characters are fishing, and one pulls out an old boot, and the next thing that happens is the other character pulls out the Loch Ness monster, then all the opportunity in between is lost, as you can't go back to normality after that big offer.

The players would have more fun if they built on the boot incrementally: for example the other

boot, socks, shirt, and so on; the players will need to figure out how this fits into the plot, which is the storytelling part of the scene and means justifying each incremental addition. By building the story slowly the players take their time, the audience will go with them, and the scene will seem more believable. Escalating too quickly is known as false heightening.

The following dialogue is an example of heightening:

Two actors in a church are playing priests:

Actor 1: 'The roof is leaking, Father, and we need to fix it – if only someone more senior were here to clear the budget!'
Actor 2: 'Yes, if only the Bishop were here!'

Enter Actor 3:

Actor 3: 'Hello, Fathers.'
Actor 1: 'Hello, Bishop Rooney: can you clear the budget so we can have the leak in the roof fixed?'
Bishop Rooney: 'If only someone more senior were here! I should call Archbishop Caretta.'

Enter Actor 4:

Actor 4: 'Hello Fathers, hello Bishop Rooney!'
All other Actors: 'Hello, Archbishop Caretta! Can you clear the budget so we can have the leak in the roof fixed?'
Archbishop Caretta: 'If only someone more senior were here! I should call Cardinal Moore!'

Enter Actor 5:

Actor 5: 'Hello Fathers, Archbishop Caretta, Bishop Rooney!'
All the other actors: 'Hello, Cardinal Moore: can you clear the budget to have the leak in the roof fixed?'
Cardinal Moore: 'If only His Holy Father were here, we could ask him!'

Enter Actor 6:

Actor 6: 'Hello Fathers, Bishops, Cardinal Moore!'
All the other actors: 'Hello, Holy Father: can you clear the budget so we can have the leak in the roof fixed?'
Holy Father: 'If only I had some divine advice! I'll pray to our Lord the Saviour!'

Enter Actor 7:

Actor 7: 'Hello Fathers, Bishops, Cardinal Moore, Tom! (Addressing the Pope by his first name should get a cheap laugh from the audience, as this character entering is obviously Jesus.)
All the other actors: (They fall to their knees.) 'Jesus our Lord and Saviour: can you clear the budget so we can have the leak in the roof fixed?'
Jesus: 'I'll need to clear it with Dad, but it should be fine!'
Booming voice from the side: 'Call Smiths and Sons, roof fitters – they did a great job on the dome in St Michael's in Camden last year, and they give a great price!'

There is then black-out.

False Heightening

Two actors in a church are playing priests:

Actor 1: 'The roof is leaking, Father, and we need to fix it – if only someone more senior were here to clear the budget!'
Actor 2: 'Yes, if only the Bishop were here!'

Enter Actor 3:

Actor 3: 'Save yourself the time lads, it's me, Jesus. All good, get Smiths and Sons, they did a great job on the dome in St Michael's in Camden and they give a great price!'

There is then black-out.

As you do this, bear in mind the following:

- In the examples above the hierarchy of the Catholic Church is used to illustrate heightening.
- In the false heightening example we lose all the fun of getting to the same ending.
- In false heightening the game is climaxed too soon, and all the fun of the game is lost.
- Where there are diminishing returns the game may not be connecting, and may need to be dropped for a new pattern. You will know this by the reaction of the audience.

USING EXTRAS AND TAGGING

There will be occasions when the players on stage or in the scene will need help from their team-mates to build the game. This can be done in several ways with extras and tagging.

Extras

Short-form improv scenes tend not to have tagging as part of the format, so the off-stage players can come in and help as extras. For example, if you have two grounded players in a scene, the extras can make short appearances to build a surreal world. Or if there is one grounded and one surreal character in the scene, the extras can come in and partner up with one or the other. Usually this works better when the extras partner up with the surreal character.

There is a mix of opinion on how long extras should stay on stage, and how much they should offer in the scene. Joining the scene and adding a single offer, then leaving, tends to work the best in short form, and also gives the other off-stage players an opportunity to jump in and escalate.

An extra can stay on longer if the scene calls for it. For example, the extra could be playing a character that the protagonists have mentioned or have been talking about. If this happens, then they have to appear, and will more than likely find a reason to stay.

Tagging

More popular in long-form improv, tagging is the tool used to move the story and open the game with even more options.

A good way to start playing with tagging and using it to find a game is as follows:

- Let a scene start.
- Onstage players find the 'who, what, where'.
- Let the scene settle to a day in the life of these characters; nothing extraordinary should happen yet.
- Once something shines out to the off-stage players, they can tag in.
- Usually they would tag out the player who made the shiny offer.
- The player left is usually the grounded character (though it doesn't have to be – the surreal character could stay and the players tagging in could be escalating the central character in a mundane world where they react as the surreal character).
- The other players will then tag in around the grounded player and escalate the situation.

Tagging is a great exercise that helps beginners or people new to finding the game to look at stories and build on situations in an incremental fashion. The important word here is 'incremental': the scene could be dramatic, but the build-up can still be slow.

The game within an improvised scene doesn't have to be funny, it can also be sophisticated and real. I recall a set of tagged scenes of two British soldiers in a World War I trench having a fairly mundane conversation about their lives at home. Both were tagged out, and the next scene portrayed their sons in a World War II situation, having almost the same conversation, but using the language of the time. These players were then also tagged out, and the same was done with the soldiers of the opposing side. The scene came to an end with four modern-day people having a similar conversation but all together, bringing the entire game to a nice closing.

In this case the scene was quite serious, as it looked at real historical events. The players were genuine in their acting, making sure not to stereotype or downplay these sad moments of

Two actors in mid-scene; the story would be set up enough so that the audience know the 'who, what, where' of the characters. It is important that we know this before we tag one out.

Tagging should be done quickly and firmly, so the new idea being brought in by the tagger can be moved quickly. If there is a delay the moment will get lost.

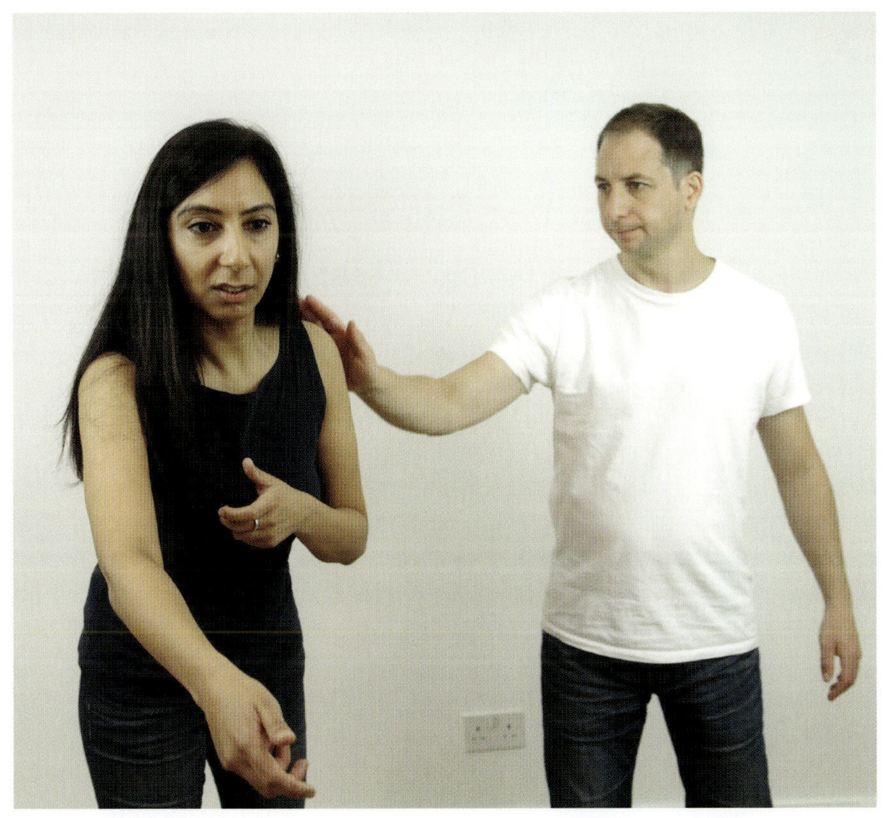

Once tagging contact has been made, the tagged player should stop what they are doing and leave the stage.

The other person in the scene who is not tagged may not be aware a tagging has happened, so should continue with what they are doing until they learn more.

history, and this really drew in those of us observing in the room. It seemed we were watching a piece of scripted theatre instead of watching an improvised story. In this scene comedy was not what happened: instead we were given a look at humanity, and how behind it all we are the same across the generations, even in times of war.

The finale then took us to the modern day where we are now in times of peace, and where people of that generation live, work and socialize together.

Even though this particular scene did have humorous moments, this was not what we remembered or took away from it. Those of us watching were far more engaged with the alignment of the states of mind of all the characters, and how the actors played it. This demonstrated that improvisation is not just for comedy, but when moments such as this happen, it can help us find the truth.

IF THERE IS NO GAME

If the Game is Blocked

It can happen that when playing, improvisers could have difficulty finding the game to catch on to. This could be caused by the players handing each other too many offers, and starting to become misaligned about what to play with. This is also known as 'overloading' the scene with information. The best way to avoid this is to play the offers like a ping-pong match. Using this approach, you will be more inclined to pay attention to each offer and to pick up a pattern within the first three to five lines.

If the Game Doesn't Happen

If it happens that a game doesn't surface, then it would be best not to force it. Instead, play the scene for what it is. If you keep to the structure and continue to make each other look good, then something will happen that will please the audience. If not a game in the conventional sense as we have discussed, you can still run a wholesome scene that the audience will enjoy.

SUMMARY

- Let the game play out naturally.
- Keep the offers simple and easy for your scene partner to say 'yes' to.
- The first thing you find is usually good enough, so play it.
- Escalate incrementally or you will burn out the game too soon.
- Find an ending, and once you hit the diminishing return, end it, or you lose the fun.

EXERCISES

The following exercises will be useful:

- Face-to-face exchange/word association
- Revolve
- Meanwhile

PROGRESS INCREMENTALLY

If you are at home flicking through the television channels and you stumble on a science-fiction or action movie, the chances are that you will keep flicking, because you don't know how the characters got to that point, and so following it from there gives you the feeling that the story you are watching is too far-fetched. The same applies with this concept if you are finding the game: if you start too high or you are too surreal the audience will have trouble believing you. So take them with you, incrementally.

- Word association
- *Seanchaí* – storyteller
- Unsuitable applicant (practise incrementally)

EVERYDAY LIFE

Once you understand how to spot, play and heighten the game, you can look for opportunities to play in your day-to-day life. Many couples and close friends have their own private jokes that they draw on at various times when the mood is right. This is a game you can cultivate by spending time together.

Can you think of any you might have devised organically with your partner or close friends?

6
MAKING THE AUDIENCE CARE

It is important to learn how to make characters believable while improvising, as we want the audience to care about them, and to believe the relationship between them. Character is also more than a funny voice, an accent and a silly way of walking. Everything an improvising actor needs to know about their character should be in the emotion they are feeling right at that moment, and the way they are reacting to the other characters and the plot or storyline.

In the conventional sense of acting the actors have a script to work from, and this gives them information they can research, and they can make character choices based on elements they have gleaned from the script. For example, they have already been provided with a storyline in which the characters have a part to play, and if any one character is a big enough player in this story, then they will have an arc to journey through. This gives the actor a lot of the information they need to build out their character.

In a situation where the character is a passing part, and does not appear often in the story,

When we think of characters, we should consider the situation they are in, and with whom. We should also consider how the situation affects the way in which an individual will act, and how they will change over the course of the interaction.

then the actor will have more work to do off-screen. Another situation could be where there are two characters who may only meet for one scene on screen, but who have more of a history or relationship than we can see. These are two examples where improvisation and traditional acting come together.

IN PRACTICE

Improvising characters in a play or film works differently from improvising in an improvised scene.

Improvising in a Play or Film

With a scripted character, character creation is not easier by any means than it is for an improviser, but it is different. In creating characters for a play or film, or any scripted piece, the information that actors may have access to are things such as:

- gender
- name
- age
- sexual orientation
- marital or relationship status
- class
- education
- occupation

The information they may *not* have are things such as:

- the history of their relationship with their immediate family members;
- how they met people they already know;
- what life was like for them in their earlier years.

This is where a director may ask actors to improvise off-script scenes to pad out these gaps. The improvised scenes may never be used in the final cut, but they give the actor a greater insight into the character they are playing.

It is also common for actors to be asked to improvise scenes that are non-scripted with the intention of these making the final cut. In this case the actor would make the maximum use of the information they already have to show how the character would react in that situation with that person at that exact time in their life.

The next layer to consider is the complexity of the human condition. As humans we can be affected by external factors, such as what is happening in a person's life at that point in time? Have they just lost their job, or a close friend or family member? Bringing all these aspects together makes a more believable character for our audience to connect and empathize with. It also gives the actor dimensions they can bring to the performance.

Improvising a Character in Improv

In the form of improv without a script, we won't have access to the information described above until the scene starts to build. So we need to be paying close attention to what offers are presented to us by our scene partners, and how we react to them. As well as paying attention to what is being offered to us, we also need to make generous offers to help build the character of our scene partner.

When the improvisers first step on to the stage they have an empty slate, which means they need to establish several factors before they can move the story forwards.

This includes establishing who the characters are, where they are, and what the relationship is between them. (As discussed in previous chapters, the characters tend to work better if they know each other.) We have called this the 'who, what, where' of the scene, and it is important not just for the audience so they can follow what's happening, but also for the actors.

It works better if the characters endow each other with attributes – this could be anything from physical attributes, such as how they look

IMPROVISATION AS AN ACTOR'S TOOL

In *Romeo and Juliet*, there is an interesting relationship between the nurse and Lady Capulet. We know that the nurse has been looking after Juliet since her birth, which means that she has been in this family's life for fourteen years or more. In the play itself, there is only one scene between Lady Capulet and the nurse, so to give these characters more depth in their relationship, the director may have the actors improvise situations not scripted.

In *Carthaginians*, by Frank McGuinness (1988), I once played the part of Seph. This character is on stage from the beginning, but he doesn't speak until halfway through scene 4. In fact he hasn't spoken a word since the events of Bloody Sunday, after which he gave up some of his friends to the RUC (Ulster Police) for joining the IRA. Seph's logic was that if they were picked up by the police, they would live, but if they joined the IRA to fight, they would almost certainly die. And after years of experiencing the Troubles, and having witnessed the deaths of thirteen innocent people on that Sunday morning, Seph had seen enough death, and so to save them, he reported them.

Seph's friends, and the other characters whom we see in this play, regard him as a traitor, but Seph himself still believes he did the right thing. The audience watching are also easily led to believe that Seph is a traitor, once they find out why he is silent – but as the actor playing this character, I needed to understand more clearly *why* Seph had done this.

To help me justify his actions the director took my character and put him in a scene with characters who do not exist in the play – namely his parents and older brother – and they confronted him as to why he had 'shopped' his friends. As this is not a scripted part of the play, involving characters who do not exist to the reader or the audience, the scenes had to be improvised. As the other characters berated mine, I had to work hard to find justification for my character's actions. Other scenes were devised and improvised with several other different people in Seph's life who also do not appear in the play, and there was an improvised scene with the character Hark, whom we do see, and who has an obvious problem with Seph and his betrayal.

The exercises provided me with the tool I needed to find my character's integrity, and to understand why he did what he did. Once I had found empathy with Seph, I was able to bring all the emotions experienced in the improvised scenes with me on to the stage. So even though he is silent for almost four scenes, Seph is still a rounded character as seen by the audience.

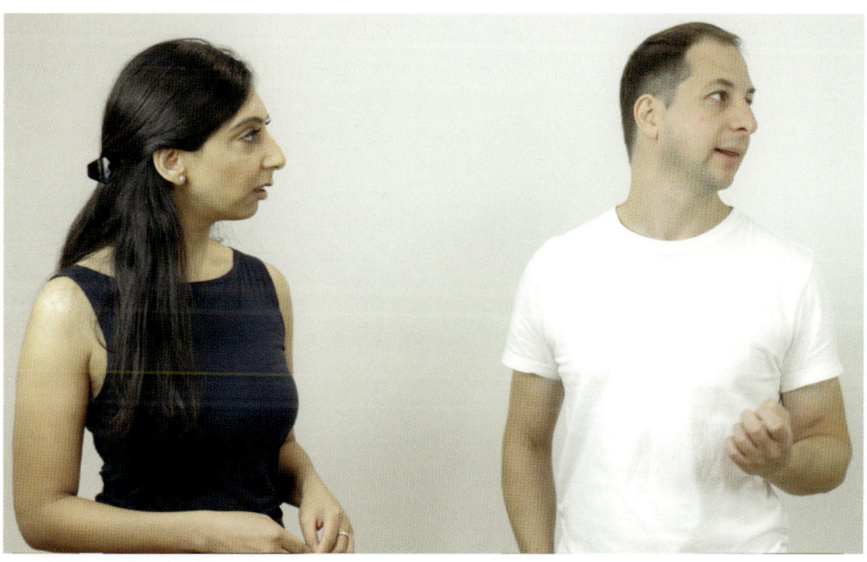

These improvisers are taking their time to get to know their characters.

These characters are slowly building on the information they have set up.

physically or emotionally, or what they might be wearing or doing.

Self-endowing at the start of a scene can still work, and it can help if actors give some history about who they are, but having characteristics endowed can be more fun for all, and is a more improvised situation, as you have less choice as to who you may become in the scene; for example:

Actor 1: 'Grandfather, it's so good to see you!'
Actor 2: 'You are such a good granddaughter to come and visit me in my old folks' home.'

At this point it would make sense if the actor playing the grandfather took on the attributes of an old man. They might decide to make their voice deeper or scratchier, or to walk with a hunchback, with an imaginary walking stick to help build on that physical feature. The person playing the granddaughter might decide to be young, in their early twenties, or middle-aged with a family of their own. These are choices that the actor can make about their own character, based on the offer they get from their scene partner.

Actors can then start to build archetypes around their character – so for example, what would be the archetypal character of the old man in an old peoples' home? More than likely he is alone, so he could be widowed or divorced, and he is living in a home because he has passed the point of being able to look after himself. He may be angry or bitter about this, or on the other hand he may be quite happy about it. Either way, this is a choice that an actor can make regarding their own character.

To give your character more dimension the actor can now raise the stakes: for example, maybe in this story the old grandfather has met someone and has decided to remarry. This may cause some turmoil with his own children, as they may fear for their inheritance and resist the idea. It will also change the whole dynamic of the scene, because instead of the grumpy old man who seemed pessimistic and bitter, now he has changed and is behaving like a love-struck teenager.

This change in direction brings a level of complexity to the characters and the scene.

As Irish actor Cillian Murphy often says when promoting his work: 'It's far more interesting to explore the complexity of the human condition.'

FINDING YOUR CHARACTER

A scene opens, and the suggestion from the audience is 'coffee shop'.

Actor 1: 'John, can you make sure the order for the office meeting in the bank across the road is ready before 1pm?'
Actor 2: 'It's almost ready Marta, I'll drop it over in ten minutes.'
Actor 1: 'Great! And are you still OK to run things tomorrow when I'm off?'
Actor 2: 'Of course, no problem! Good luck at the food fair. I hope you find something interesting we can add to our menu.'

In the above 'who, what, where' example, these actors have established some of the facts we need to build on their characters:

- Names/gender (assuming the names John/ Marta are perceived as male/female).
- Status (who the boss is).
- What is happening right now, and in general in the life of these characters.

There are also some assumptions the actors can make about themselves and those in the scene with them:

- John is Marta's most trusted colleague or worker; or maybe their relationship is more than that (siblings, business partners or a couple)?
- Marta is looking for something new to add to the menu.

If the actors take the plot that the restaurant is in trouble, how would this affect the characters?

- Marta might be irritable or stressed.
- John might be the same, or he might offer the voice of reason.

Either way, the feelings the characters have can be taken by the actors to develop the characters further, as everything they need to know about the 'who' they are playing is revealed to them as the dialogue continues.

In this scene, the actors will further raise the stakes and tell us what is at stake so the audience will care more about the characters.

Actor 1: 'When Mum and Dad left this place to us, we promised them we would do our best to keep it going, so it could be handed down to another generation.'
Actor 2: 'Yes, but times are hard since the big coffee chains moved in two blocks down.'

Here the actors may take on emotions of loyalty to their family legacy, and bitterness towards a growing franchise.

We have all watched films and television shows with situations similar to this, and we always take the side of the underdog – and if the actors play the truth of the emotions that such characters would feel in this situation, they will bring a level of connection between the audience and the characters.

Archetypes and Stereotypes (Dos and Don'ts)

Without getting into the psychology of archetypes and stereotypes, the best way to see how these can be used for improv is to look at how an archetype presents itself. The presentation of certain types of character gives the actor a start as to how they can initially present their character,

ARCHETYPES AND STEREOTYPES

Some examples of archetypes:

- hero
- explorer
- sage (wise oracle)
- leader (spiritual or physical)
- joker/entertainer
- rebel
- artist
- explorer
- lover
- caregiver
- warrior

Some examples of stereotypes:

- father – authoritative
- mother – loving and caregiving
- grandfather – could also be authoritative and wise, and act more like a mentor
- grandmother – could be an amplified version of a mother
- police officer – could be stern and ask direct questions
- cook or a chef – busy and decisive
- judge – someone who is very wise
- doctor – holds the moral high ground
- artist – inspired by everything, or a tortured soul
- sportsperson – confident and strong

until they find out more about who they are and where the story is going.

Using an archetype as a way to get your character up and running is useful, and more fun can be had when you begin to combine them with a stereotype – for example, you could be playing a father who is also a tortured artist, or a mother who is a police officer. Combining these behaviours into a single complex character can be fun for the actor. So start off as an archetypal mother who is loving and caring, and add the layer of her being a police officer. Now you are starting to build a complex character right on the spot.

The character's morals, and what they want right in that moment when we meet them, will be defined in the dialogue.

Making the Character Personal

We need to make a character personal so the audience can connect with the person portrayed: they need to understand what that character's core values and morals are.

If you were portraying a football captain, then the attributes that you could take to this character are leadership, both spiritual and physical; also of a sage, who is wise and experienced; and of a warrior. Add to this the stereotype of a sportsperson who is strong and confident, and this is a very good start. But why does this character want to win this football match? What are the values that drive this ambition? Is it a family legacy? Do they want to do it to impress a lover, or is it just to be popular? Maybe it is a genuine love of the sport, so they want to lead their team to success. This will be discovered and portrayed through the dialogue that they have with their scene partner.

Helping the Other Actors Build on their Characters

It is a good trait of an improviser to give information back to their scene partner and help them build on their character. They can do this by adding to their background. Let's go back to the example of the sportsman.

Actor 1: 'Good training session tonight, John. I'm confident that we will take the trophy next Sunday.'

Actor 2: 'The team are all confident, too. That speech you gave at the end of training was really inspiring. Was it the same speech Dad made when he was captain?'

These improvisers are endowing each other's characters in order to build their background.

Improvisers make solid eye contact as their characters build tension.

Actor 1: 'Yes, it was. I was just a kid when I saw him stand in this dressing room and make it, and it's been a dream of mine to captain this side when I came of age. And to have my younger brother with me is a real honour.'

Actor 2: 'Me too, Charlie, that provincial trophy has made it home to the Murphy home for four generations, always captained by one of us.'

Character Exercises

My favourite character-building exercise to get a quick physical identity is known to me as 'follow a body part'. My real-life default tends to be my left shoulder; I never noticed until it was pointed out in an acting class years later, but I've seen two characters with the same physical identity, probably a coincidence, but noticeably to me.

The first was the character of Tommy, played by Tom Hardy, in *Warrior*. He is an ex-marine with a history of competitive fighting. I have no idea how Tom Hardy built this particular character, it was just an observation I made when enjoying the film.

The other example is a character played by Eddie Redmayne in *Fantastic Beasts and Where to Find Them*. The character leads with his left shoulder, and to me was very prominent. Again, I have no idea how Eddie Redmayne cultivated this character. I usually tell this story as an overview before I start the exercise with the group.

The exercise itself is to ask the group to walk around the room in a neutral fashion in any direction. Take heed of what body part may be leading them naturally, and what in their past could have triggered this.

Once they have worked out to some degree what in their past could be driving the way they carry themselves, I remind them to keep their thoughts clear again, and for now to avoid eye contact with each other. I then ask them to think about a character, basing it on whoever they want – a friend, uncle, aunt, old schoolteacher.

Then detached from that actual person, begin to cultivate a past for them. Think about where they grew up, how they grew up. What kind of social class did they come from, are their parents still together? Were their parents together when they were growing up? How many siblings do they have, where do they come in the family order, and how does that affect them?

Now consider what part of their body might take a lead. What kind of personality are they, are they a dominant alpha type? Are they strong, confident, sexy, or are they shy, maybe a bit insecure? Start pulling these things together, and begin to express it in the way you walk around. Now name your character: are you married, divorced, engaged? In love, or recently broken up? Maybe you don't believe in marriage and you have a long-term partner. Or you could be single. Now begin to take notice of the people around you. Make eye contact and acknowledge each other. Nod, smile and say hello if you want. Now imagine you are at a wedding. Who do you know there? Are you a guest of the bride or groom?

As you speak to each other, try and remember as much as you can about the other people.

Once the group has spent several minutes chatting in character, pick two at a time and give them a scene to run. If the group are beginners, then it can be helpful to load the scene with as much information as possible. Give them a 'who, what, where'; 'who' means how they know each other – for example, the posh uncle of the groom would also be the uncle of the groom's sister, who is an aspiring singer–songwriter. So tell them where they are, and why they are there. Then let them run the scene. You can side coach, and remind them to react as their characters.

This can be run with all levels – the more advanced the group, the less scene filling you can give them. The exercise is to remind people to think as their character would – so if you are a hen-pecked office worker whose general outlook on life is poor, then keep to that. Encourage the players to act, and more importantly react to the situation they are in within the scene.

One character gives
an object to another
character.

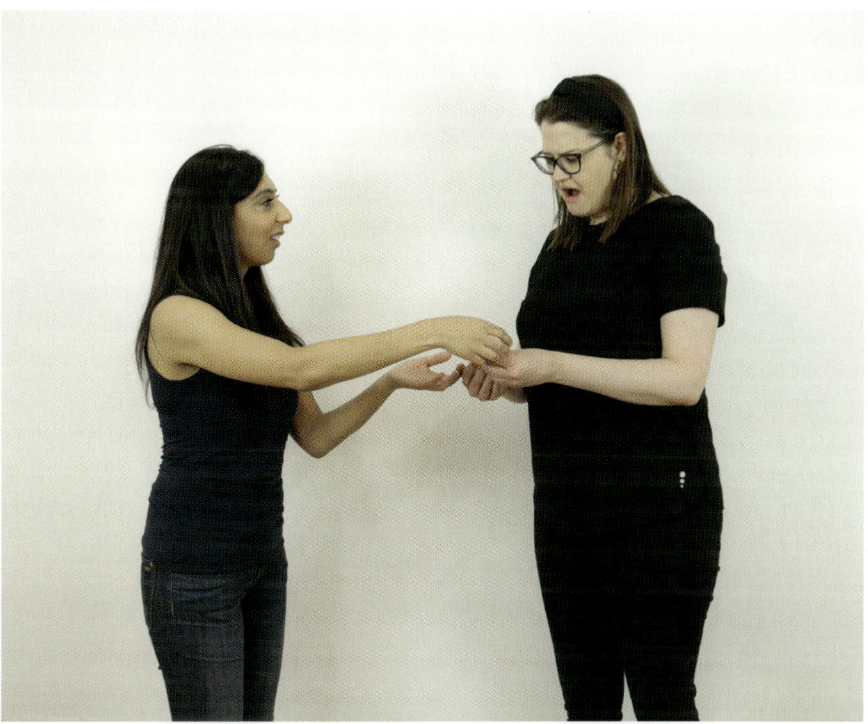

The response is not as
expected.

An improviser makes a verbal offer to another improviser.

BELOW: The response is not as expected, and this adds dimension to the characters.

CHARACTER DIMENSION

All of us to a certain extent live a dual existence – not to the extreme of Superman or Wonder Woman, but there is a different version of us depending on the circumstances and the environment. A duality easier for us to comprehend would be of a more human day-to-day character, such as Tony Soprano. In the series, one of the themes is the fact that he has two families: his immediate family with his wife and children, and then his business family. The obvious difference between these versions of himself is his behaviour, depending on who is in his company – and the overlap can come and go between them, also. For example, Tony has a paternal mentor relationship with his nephew Christopher, and in this situation shows his fathering side even if he is amongst his mafia friends.

His more sinister side comes to the surface when he is dealing with material things, and especially with his sister Janice and his wife Carmela. His conflict with Janice centres round the ownership and use of their mother's house, and with Carmela when they are having conversations about separating.

If we only ever saw Tony's mafia side, we would be missing a big part of his values. This also gives the character different dimensions.

Having characters that are open to change depending on the situation is important, so in an improvised scene it will always make more sense for the protagonists to have been impacted by the other characters. This shows us that they are human and gives the character different dimensions.

Character Status

Defining a character's status can really help an improviser achieve a firm holding in a scene. Status in our day-to-day lives is always changing, and depending on where you are and with whom you are speaking, your status can change. For example, in your place of work and while discussing a work-related topic with your manager, the higher status would be with the more senior person (senior in terms of role). However, if you put the same characters in a different situation, such as in a social gathering where there is no work being discussed, the status could swap: this time it could be that the manager is less well known in the bar or restaurant they are in, and may not be well versed in the topic of conversation they are having.

RECOGNIZING STATUS

Status can be defined in the opening few lines of a scene, and you can either make or accept the offer for it. If you look around you in your daily life, you can see status between people everywhere. Some people share equal status, such as couples or siblings, but this could switch, depending on the topic of conversation. In the opening of a scene when the improvisers are setting up the 'who, what, where', status will be embedded in this. You could get two players to try this out; for example:

Actor 1: 'Fourth floor please, Mike.'
Actor 2: 'Good morning, Mr Grady. Big finance meeting today then?'
Actor 1: 'Yes. Sorry I missed your stand-up comedy gig last night. I had to prepare for the meeting.'
Actor 2: 'Not to worry, we had a fun night. Good reaction. Thanks for asking.'
Actor 1: 'Well, it's only a matter of time before you can give up operating elevators and become famous! I'll be sure to come see you at the comedy club Saturday night!'

In this scene, we have a person who seems to be a businessman of some kind (the details are as yet undefined) and the elevator operator. The characters know each other, and the individual of higher status here would be Mr Grady, where Mike, who works in the service industry, would be the lower. However, the status would swap if we see the same characters in the comedy club where Mike performs his stand-up routine.

STATUS EXERCISE: PLAYING CARDS

In order to get the idea of status into the heads of your students, this is a very popular exercise:

- Use a group of ten people, and give each a playing card with a number between 1 and 10, 10 being of highest status and 1 the lowest.
- They should hold the card against their forehead, and should not know themselves what number they are.
- Ask the improvisers to walk round the room and interact with each other.
- Treat the person they are speaking to with the status that matches the card the other has held to their forehead.
- They should not directly reveal the number the other is holding – all hints of status should be embedded in the form of dialogue.
- After several minutes, ask them to line up in the order they think they are in.

Most times this comes very close, if not exactly right.

Now ask the group how they were able to work it out. Those with the higher numbers usually report that they seemed to be popular, and that most people in the room wanted to speak with them. So they played the tactic of being popular, and getting attention from the other popular people in the exercise, as they figured out their numbers were close together. Then something interesting starts to happen, because as the groups break apart into smaller groups, the status of the card number begins to surface. The highest numbered person starts being treated with the most respect and attention, while the lowest with the least. If you leave it to play out for several minutes, the group will work this out for themselves.

Often as the activity is playing out, the group breaks into three smaller groups, which align themselves: these tend to be 1 to 4, 5 to 7 and 8 to 10. These mini groups work out their own status order, and when you ask the full group of ten to line up in order it happens very quickly.

Follow up this exercise by having the players run short scenes using the status appointed to them by the card; then at some point, find a reason to switch it.

SUMMARY

- For improvised characters make sure you know *who* you and your scene partner are (character relationship is key).
- Take offers from your scene partner to build on your physicality.
- Try not to self-endow too much at the start of the scene, but let your scene partner gift it to you.
- If you know who you are, use an archetype to get settled.
- Using a stereotype is useful, but don't force it.
- Avoid offensive stereotyping.

BRINGING IT ALL TOGETHER

Bringing all these skills together into a single performance can seem intimidating to beginners – that no matter how much you learn and apply, there is still more to improve on. The good news is that this is the case with anything in life, and no matter how long you have been practising this art form or any other, there is always something you don't yet know.

If you find as you begin a scene that you are thinking about 'who, what, where' and 'Yes, and…', then be sure to remember your own name and that of the other character, and drive a storyline. Also you need to remember to keep your space work consistent. You may overwhelm yourself, but don't worry. The truth is that realistically this is too much for anyone to take on all at once, so instead, take your time and focus on one or two things at a time.

Which ones are up to you. If you have a quick-witted personality, you may find fun in the 'Yes, And…' and be a joy to work with because you tend to give consistent and solid offers. If you are good at being physical, then good space work may be where you find the fun. If you are technically minded and like structure, then you may like establishing the 'who, what, where'.

Whatever your strength is, when you start out, enjoy this aspect. Observe your fellow classmates and troupe members, and make a mental note of what it is you like about them, and how you could adopt something from their style. Make this your goal for the next set of classes or the rehearsal you are attending, and once you have adopted some of the techniques as second nature, you can choose another one, and so on. It can take some time to become proficient in all the necessary skills, and everyone is different.

Avoid comparing yourself to others in your community, especially your peers. We are all different, and improvisation is an opportunity for you to show your own individuality, and in time to grow new skills.

You might find on occasion that you fall into diminishing returns, or hit a plateau and feel that you are not improving, and feel a lot of frustration – but don't give up, because this will pass. Talk to your teacher or director, and ask for pointers on what you could work on. Chat with your fellow performers after classes, rehearsals or shows, and find out what you did well, and what not so well. Humility is a great way to keep yourself keen, and eager to learn and improve.

Embrace all the feedback – and most importantly, enjoy yourself!

- Think of a character's motivation in the scene (their values and behaviour).
- Make your scene partner look good.

EVERYDAY LIFE

The following tips about creating characters may be useful:

- Observe the people around you: how do they act and react? What about them can you take to your improv? Some improvisers use people from their own real life, such as parents, grandparents, aunts, uncles, friends and so on, as inspiration for their characters.
- As in real life, a character's behaviour is led by their values. What does this person think of the world, and how do they react to it?
- A person whose behaviour doesn't honour their values could be said to be of weak character.

EXERCISES

- Follow a body part on to the stage and let it influence your character.
- Choose a state of mind and let it influence your character.
- Play status playing cards.
- Endow others with an attribute.

7
IMPROV BEYOND THE STAGE

The skills of improvisation are essentially transferable, and can be used in day-to-day life; furthermore the exercises and game playing can help people in their personal and professional lives. As an art form, improv is a great way to explore your creativity and to help you begin to trust your instincts. When it comes to using it in real life, there should be no difference. The confidence gained by taking part in an improv class will begin to serve you day to day.

People join improvisation classes for many reasons; one of the most common is that they wish to work on their self-confidence, and to address some shortfall they see in their personality, which is holding them back either professionally or personally. For some it's a fear of public speaking, whether that is presenting to their colleagues at work or speaking to their boss about an idea they have, or even something as simple as entertaining people at a dinner party or walking into a bar. For others it could be thinking on the spot and being spontaneous, or it could be just to meet new people and have fun.

Whatever the reason, joining an improvisation class is a great way to improve yourself.

IN PRACTICE

As an improv student I learnt some useful techniques that helped me to overcome my fear of speaking in front of people, also to listen attentively, and to ask driving questions, making statements that could lead to decisive actions.

All these aspects came together for me through various improv classes, styles and teachers.

As with anything, the skills of improvisation are exactly that: skills! And they need to be practised in the same way as anything that you want to perfect. Not everyone who is practising improvisation is doing it to be in shows regularly, or looking for fifteen minutes of fame.

Many people take up improv and progress to the level of performance, and do their first live improv show in front of an audience of family and friends. Then once they have achieved that, they drop out. Maybe at this point they feel they have addressed the reason they took it up in the first place, and are ready to move on. This is like someone who at some point in their life trains for and runs a half- or a full marathon. They don't continue to run marathons as they have achieved the level of fitness they wanted, and also their goal of running the race, and are now content with maintaining that fitness by running 5km a couple of times a week.

Students might equate improv to going to the gym. When you go to the gym you would exercise different parts of your body on each day. So one day you work on your arms, another day on your legs, another on your chest, and so on; furthermore every trip to the gym would also include some cardiovascular exercise such as a run or a cycle, along with a warm-up and cool-down.

Improv training is much the same – so on one day you might work on your storytelling, on the next on characters, and the next on your space work. And every day you would run scenes bringing everything together so that you can practise them all together, making them second nature.

A football team would train in a similar way: they would run drills and different play sets, and finish up with a game to bring all these together. Then match day would be the equivalent of an improv show.

ON STAGE AND OFF STAGE

The difference between 'on stage' and 'off stage' might seem obvious, but what in fact are the actual differences? To be 'off stage' means exactly that: you are standing in the wings of the stage out of the light, and not disturbing the people who are centre stage. As much as you may want to be on stage, it is good practice to remember that the stage is to be shared, and in improv we are always working as an ensemble. There is never a single star of the show: we are all extras.

The same concepts are there when we are 'on stage in life'. By this we don't mean actually on stage necessarily – we mean it as an analogy for situations in which a person could be the centre of attention, or where they want to be the centre of attention.

On Stage

Being 'on stage' includes situations such as public speaking, or for those who are members of a board or committee, presenting to clients or colleagues in their place of work, either to a large group or to their team. It could also be a single one-to-one meeting, for example presenting ideas to their manager or asking them for a rise. Other situations outside professional work might include hosting a dinner party, going on a first date, or even just walking into a bar. These are all situations where the individual would be presenting their best self.

Improvisation gives skills and confidence to people, which they can take into their daily lives.

Having an on-stage mindset to fall back on will give you a set of skills to use. It also gives you the confidence you need to be in that situation.

As an on-stage persona you would observe the following behaviour:

- Keep the feet forward and stay facing the crowd: they want to see you. This is a concept that may not always work in certain meeting rooms or environments, so position yourself as best you can to be facing most people. You can also make a point that you are trying to keep the people in the wings included.
- If the on-stage situation is one to one, then face the person or sit opposite them.
- Maintain good eye contact, as this tells the person you are speaking with that you are being honest.
- Good eye contact is reflective, which means that the person you are speaking to will respond with an equal level of eye contact. This subconsciously drives listening.
- Poor eye contact gives the impression that you have something to hide.
- Keep your body language open so people feel invited in.
- Stay grounded, plant your feet firmly on the ground.
- When you move, move with purpose. Use the stage if there is space to use, and when you go to another spot on the stage, be purposeful.
- Stay calm and appear confident and competent – even if you are struggling, never let the audience know. If you stay calm, the answer will come. Trust yourself!
- Be present, trust yourself, and know that your improvisation skills of dealing with the unexpected will save you.

Off Stage

An off-stage persona, on the other hand, might display an obvious set of behaviours – such as crashed out on the sofa watching television, or in a situation where they are just an observer. However, they could be in a situation where the stage may call, and then their off-stage persona should be on stand-by.

An example of being off stage in a personal sense is being out for dinner or drinks with a group of friends and sharing stories – and if you share a story with someone, they may need to call you in to help retell it. In a personal setting the stakes may be lower.

In a professional situation it is a good skill to have. If you are presenting with a co-worker, you may be co-facilitating with someone where you have a shared set of items to present, and so you would both have times when you would be off stage for a part. Imagine you and your co-worker are presenting a big pitch to a client. It has been well prepared and rehearsed, and you are both ready, with the presentation shared: to the client it looks spontaneous, and as if you are feeding off each other. Then you notice that your co-facilitator has drawn a blank! It could be nervousness, or stage fright on the big day, but that second of silence feels like a lifetime. Luckily you are already in your off-stage persona and ready to jump in and save the day.

As an off-stage persona you would observe the following behaviour:

- Your body language should be relaxed yet attentive, paying close attention to what is happening on stage.
- Respect the person who is centre stage, and make sure you don't interrupt, or try and take the stage away from them.
- Wait to be invited, unless it is clear it is time for you to jump in.
- Avoid leaning against a wall, or if you are sitting, be sure to sit up straight so you are ready to jump in when required.
- Leaning or slouching can cost you valuable milliseconds when you are needed, and may even be the cause of you losing the moment.
- You are there to support, but only if needed, or if you are invited to the stage. You need to

remember that being centre stage is scary for some people: they are under pressure, and can feel safer when they know they have an ally off stage to support them.

- If the moment arises that you are needed, you will be able to pick up the pieces quickly.

THE SKILLS OF IMPROVISATION IN EVERYDAY LIFE

'Yes, And…' in the Workplace

The basics of offer and accept were discussed in Chapter 2, 'Yes, And…'. How does this translate to your everyday life? Using 'Yes, and…' is very collaborative, and can really drive a collaborative work environment, particularly if you think about a brainstorming exercise where you and your colleagues are working through new ideas for solving a problem.

The pushback here from a corporate perspective is that 'Yes, and…' is a great tool when being creative in the arts, but in the real world we need to be more realistic. I agree there is some truth to this, but the way forwards is to apply 'Yes, and…' when it works, and move on when it doesn't. A good facilitator with some practice will be able to identify when it will work or not. For example:

- Bring all the team together in a room or conference call.
- Outline or frame up the problem or issues you are there to solve; this could also be a kick-off meeting for a new project or programme.
- Use a flip chart of whiteboard to capture ideas.
- Build on each of these ideas. Using 'Yes, and…' here will:
  - Highlight why certain approaches won't work or may be difficult
  - Identify dependencies and stakeholders for a project

- Bring all team members together in a safe collaborative environment
- Give everyone a chance to participate (the facilitator should help drive this)
- If you use 'Yes, and…' for this brainstorming and problem solving, you will come out of the meeting with a single focus and agreement from all, which brings the team together.
- It's fun and energizing.

Thinking on your Feet

One of the first qualities that people recognize when they talk about improvisers is their ability to think on their feet. Non-improvisers equate this with a natural ability for quick thinking and good wit. For some people who are improvisers, this is the case, and they are privileged with the gift of quick thinking – but this skill can be trained for and practised.

As we discussed in Chapter 4, Spontaneity and Listening, trusting your instincts and being brave enough to speak out when the thought comes to you gets easier the more you do it. Start with topics you are comfortable with – that could be politics, history, music, sport, certain aspects of your work, or any other hobbies or interests. When the moment is there, go for it, and get used to speaking out with your point of view. Starting with things you are comfortable with will give you the confidence to move to other topics, and will improve your conversational skills.

One great piece of advice is 'be willing to have a discussion you know you are going to lose'. This has two advantages: it gives you humility by admitting you always have things to learn; and it gets you to a place where you ask questions to learn, instead of as a challenge. This makes the person you are speaking with relax and engage instead of going on the defensive.

Improvisation and Mental Health

Improvisation is a great way for a person to put themselves outside their comfort zone. And because it is a creative and safe space, students can indulge in this at low risk.

As discussed earlier, one of the key skills to master as an improviser is the ability to get to and stay in the moment. When we do this, all our worries and anxieties temporarily fade away and we enjoy the creative experience as it happens. Therefore, people when they leave an improv session feel happy and energized.

The level of support amongst a group of improvisers is unique, and difficult to replicate in any other group. For many people, improvisation is a scary thing to do as it is completely unknown, and it is not unusual for beginners to get a little anxious about doing it. But soon you learn that any mistake is a gift, and an improviser can take that gift and begin to turn it into something concrete, meaning that anything you say is the right thing and the situation can always be worked out.

One of our greatest fears as humans is that of being judged in a bad light, especially by strangers. This fear of rejection can lead people to hold back on thoughts or comments when in a discussion or conversation. The anxiety caused by these situations will lead people to be more into themselves, and to avoid people, places or situations where they may need to have to speak out and justify themselves and make an impression.

This can also lead to a loss of self, and may cause people to project a persona they think others expect. In improv people might do what normally they would not do in a controlled and low-risk environment, yet will still be happy with the outcome. Here we have a situation of life imitating art, and vice versa.

I have 0 per cent control over how people feel or react, and 100 per cent control over how I react to them. (Colette Moran BAS and Vera Wagner, MACBT, MIACP.)

ONLINE: VIRTUAL IMPROV

The outbreak of the Covid-19 pandemic in 2020 changed the landscape of theatre forever. For the first time, as far as I am aware, improvisation moved into a virtual online world with players sitting or standing in their homes and improvising with their teams. For an art form that depends so much on human interaction, we've had no choice but to embrace it. And many improvisation groups around the world have done just this in the form of shows and classes. And even as we sit in lockdown and dream of the days we spent together in small theatres and above and below pubs in London, New York, Chicago, Sydney and Dublin, and hope to have this experience again, there is a good chance and opportunity that this new virtual improvisation may stay around into the future regardless.

One of the great things for myself and the *Livewired* comedy improv troupe that I play with and direct was the additional exposure that virtual shows brought to us. For years my friends and family in Ireland have been saying 'I must get over to London and see one of your shows' – and now they can do it from the comfort of their own homes. Obviously it takes time for all of us to get used to a change of medium like this. Students, players and audience all have a different experience ahead of them when they log into an improv show or class or rehearsal and, usually, low expectations. Nevertheless, although there is still a lot to learn, I think it's worth sharing what it has been like.

Any improviser would look at this situation as an opportunity and a gift, rather than as a challenge, and would come up with ways to deal with it. In the virtual world we now experience, many of the human cues we rely on for communication are gone, and so we need to optimize those we have left.

Actors using virtual space to interact with each other.

General Virtual Best Practices

It can take some time to get used to virtual presence in practice, and if we put some important things in place in advance, we can make a big difference to those we are interacting with.

HAVE A GOOD WORKING SPACE

If possible it is a much more comfortable experience for you if you can have a dedicated working space, even if this is at your dining-room table. Make sure it is free of clutter, and that you have a comfortable chair that you can get out of easily and quickly if you need to; also make sure that your laptop or PC is plugged in or fully charged.

A laptop or a PC tends to be a better option than a tablet or a phone, especially if you are the one managing the conference software that is being used.

Keep the background as bright and as clear as possible.

HAVE A BLANK OR NON-DISTRACTIVE BACKGROUND

All our favourite television personalities now conduct conference calls from their homes, and although it is interesting to try and make out what may be on the bookshelf behind them, for the best chances of a good performance it is better to have the background blank if possible to avoid distraction.

MAINTAIN GOOD EYE CONTACT

Maintaining good eye contact is a tough ask, especially when we are not together: how can you make eye contact when no one is in front of you? Well, the truth of it is that you will have to cheat. Keeping eye contact with the camera gives the impression to the others that you are engaged, as you are focusing centrally. One way to help with this is to have your laptop or camera at eye level. Use phone books, cookbooks or boxes for this purpose – just make sure they are stable.

When acting with other players, you will need to look at the screen to see what they are doing, and to have a connection with your scene partner.

Give the illusion of eye contact by looking in the direction of your on-screen scene partner.

Have Good Lighting

You don't need to have professional lighting, but you do need to make sure that your face is lit appropriately. Avoid too much light behind you, as this will darken your features, which we need to see if you are acting. Also try to avoid light reflecting on your screen, as this will be a problem for people who are trying to see you. The best place to have a light is above and behind your laptop or PC so it is on your face but out of the camera shot. A strong desk lamp tends to be enough.

Headphones may be recommended but can be cumbersome when trying to act. You will have a better experience if you can find a quiet place in your home where you will not be subject to disturbance.

As best you can, continue to keep eye contact.

Be aware of how your device will appear on the viewer's screen.

KNOW YOUR SOFTWARE

You need to be familiar with the conference app you are using, and should consider the following:

- What features will you need?
- Will you be using any media, pictures or videos?
- Will it be necessary for people not to hear or see what's happening for a period of time: think about short-form guessing games, where the main player would leave the room for several moments while the game is set up.
- How will you interact with your audience? Verbally or via a chat or messaging function?
- Is there a limit to who can be seen, or who can access the conference?
- What limitations can you give to the audience so they can't disrupt things?

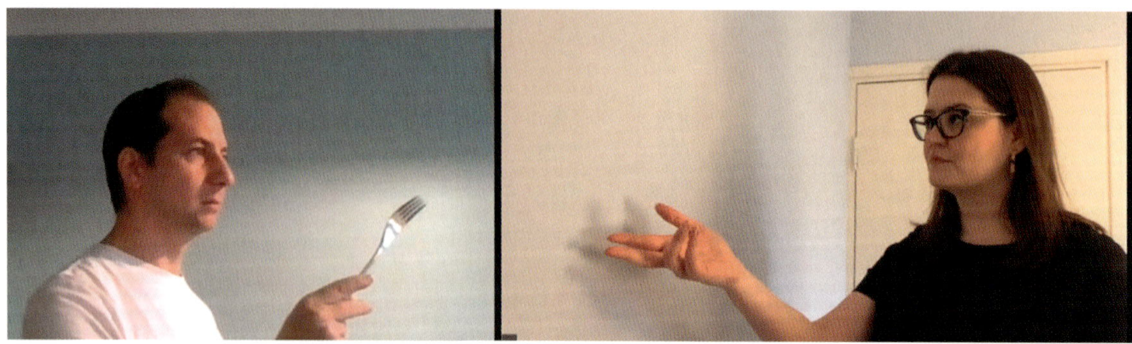

Use the illusion of space by passing objects between improvisers.

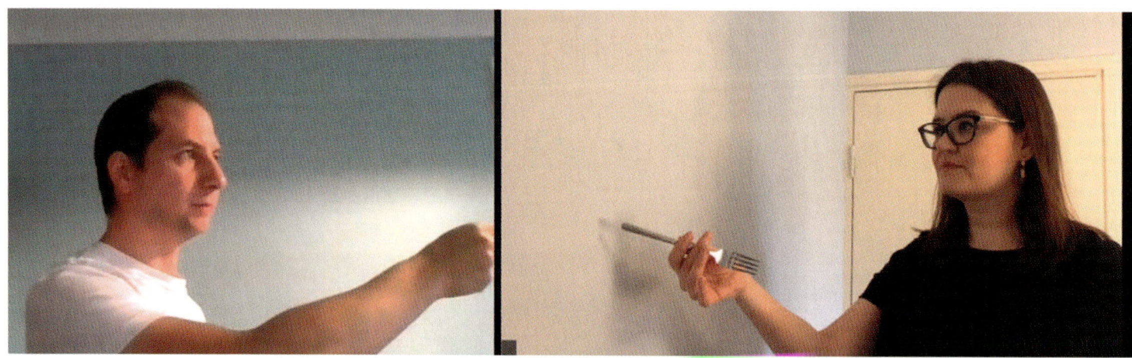

If done well, with some practice, a virtual set-up can be very effective in creating the illusion that the players are together, and will help with player chemistry.

• What additional measures can the host(s) have to keep control?

Running a Virtual Rehearsal or Class

Greet everyone individually – it's not like a room, where people can pair up and say hello; a new group will look to the teacher to feel safe straight away.

Create an imaginary circle, and give everyone a unique number (if there are twelve of you, give each person a number between one and twelve); then in sequence have everyone call their number (one, two, three, four, and so on). Repeat this a few times so everyone can get the feeling of who follows who. Also try it backwards. What you have done here is create a virtual circle.

Next switch to first names, and speed it up. This will help people focus. You can use this structure to play one-word games, such as a one-word story or poem.

You can also try some across-the-circle warm-up games. Maybe something simple, such as word association: call a person's name, then a noun – for example 'Barbara' – 'milk'. Barbara will then repeat the word received and call another person, who will then add a word associated with milk: for example 'milk – Bob: cow'; 'cow – Maria: farm', and so on. It can be slow to start with, but stay with it. Once the game picks up pace more complex associations can be tried.

If people are experienced stage performers, get them to slow down when speaking as the technology tends to create a barrier as well as a time delay.

Virtual players need to:

• listen more attentively
• speak more clearly and allow for delay in delivery
• be more focused so they can be engaged

Running a Virtual Show

Many big improv groups have taken up the challenge and are putting on virtual shows. The obvious difference is that we no longer have an audience in front of us to let us know if we are doing a good job. Nevertheless there are several ways you can interact with your audience. For example, use the chat function in the conference app – though this could be difficult to do in parallel if you are hosting a show. It could therefore help to have a co-host, whose job is to keep the conversation going when the host is between acts, and to be a helping hand with the technology.

It is important to make sure you keep good relations with your audience throughout. Another way to do this is to 'unmute' them, and get them to interact with you directly. There is a danger that the unmuting can cause feedback and disrupt the entire show, but this is where your co-host can help, by looking after the technological side of things.

Interactive conversations with the audience make them feel more a part of the show: it builds a friendlier environment and gives the feeling of it being a live show. It also takes some of the pressure off the host, because you now have something to banter with.

It is important to maintain good relations and engagement with the audience throughout. Keep checking in with them. I found that 'unmuting' and having short conversations with people worked very well.

8

TEACHING, COACHING AND DIRECTING

Although there are some overlaps between the three roles of teaching, coaching and directing, they do have differences, and a teacher, a coach and a director need to be aware of these in order to give good feedback to players. Also, for players leading a group or directing a rehearsal, or who are devising new games or formats, it is good to know when to use aspects from which discipline.

I am often asked: 'How do you teach improv – isn't it all made up on the spot?' or 'How can you direct improv – isn't that a contradiction in terms?' The short answer to this is, of course, yes! But don't confuse teaching and directing improv with directing a play or a television piece from a script. Directing is not about telling the actors what to do, it's more about guiding them with the whole artistic vision in mind. In improvisation, directing is not about getting players ready for a situation, it's about getting your players ready for *any* situation by keeping their skills sharp.

TEACHING

With teaching for anything, it is hard not to observe Maslow's hierarchy of needs to help students get to where they need to be in order to learn. Immediate needs might include having a comfortable space to learn in, with a good ambient temperature, and encouraging people to wear appropriate clothing and footwear that they can move around in. Providing water and appropriate breaks is also important, as is creating a safe space for all by finding out

people's expectations – not everyone in the room is there to be in show business: they could be there for personal reasons. If you discover that people are feeling intimidated, or feel they don't belong, you should address this.

Work to create an inclusive feel: it is out of your control who turns up, but be aware if there is any imbalance in gender, race or language, and address this to make sure that everyone feels they belong there. If these criteria can all be put in place, then students will get to a point where they surprise themselves with what they can do.

Regarding content, start at the beginning with a brief history, and then describe the various theories and best practices already given in this book. It is important for the teacher to be familiar and experienced with the different aspects, and to be able to draw on some examples from their time spent on stage, or when and where certain things worked and others didn't.

As many teachers will probably tell you, students want to break the rules straight away, and there is nothing wrong with that – it shows great enthusiasm for being creative and wanting to improvise – but it's better to break the rules when you understand them. The advantage of knowing and understanding the rules first, and being able to apply them, brings you to a higher level of evaluation and ultimately creation. This is better known as Bloom's 'Taxonomy Hierarchy of Learning', and is as applicable to the education of improvisation as it is to anything academic.

For an improviser to be creative in an artistic way, and to one day create original and entertaining games and formats, there needs to be a foundation of knowledge that they can use to 'unpack' the work of others. This way there is a disruption process happening for the player, as they push the boundaries and formulate their own creative process – which is very personal for each player.

As a teacher moves through their own curriculum, the students start to pick up the various skills. This is when the teacher will use some old-fashioned feedback, based on the behaviour of the players. Mostly new improvisers are not sure if what they are doing is right, so it is the teacher's job to help them recognize when they are sparking their creative process and coming up with great improvised moments. This is best done in the form of praise, and positive reinforcement. It can also help if there is a competition element to the game or exercise.

If a new improviser captures a moment of emotion that is believable for the character they are playing, it is important for the teacher to call it out and praise it. Hopefully this will help the student form a creative process for replication, so they do it again. How the student does it is not really any of the teacher's business, as this is personal to each individual – and as artists, it can take time for each of us to find our own way. In the same way that a stand-up comedian or singer–songwriter takes time to find their voice, an improviser needs time to find their 'funny'.

When a teacher gives critical feedback is mostly based on when and where a student would flout the rules and maybe sabotage the scene. This could occur if they block an offer, or fail to pick up the game, or any other skill taught in the curriculum. Of course, the teacher needs to be a step ahead, and to be aware of where the students may be going so as not to make assumptions, and so they don't give feedback on the scene they wanted to see, or would have done.

A good follow-up is for the teacher to find a way that will help the students to remember the lesson or feedback. Several people have used well-known sitcom or scenes in films so students have a way to recall it, or have even gone and watched it in order to confirm the feedback.

In beginner scenes a trainer/trainee or mentor/protégé relationship is quite often seen. This is a very interesting relationship to explore, but what tends to happen with beginners is that it turns into a teaching scene, which means the story gets stuck. This is because the teacher has full control of the scene, and it ends up with them ordering the other player around the stage.

I use the relationship between Rocky Balboa and his manager Mickey (played by Sylvester Stallone and Burgess Meredith respectively) in *Rocky I*, *II* and *III* to cement this feedback. The core of the relationship is not the training and Mickey demanding more push-ups, even though this does happen: there is much more between these characters, and this is revealed in the dialogue. This search for the truth is much more interesting to see, such as Mickey's past as a boxer and trainer, and Rocky's aspirations to be the best.

It is also good to give the students space to discuss their perspective on the feedback, as this is not a binary art form and there is no right or wrong answer; therefore encouraging discussion gives the students a chance to air and understand their own perspectives.

COACHING

Coaching improvisation differs from teaching it, because at this point in the students' journey they probably have a good grasp of the rules and best practices. The task of the coach is therefore to help the players explore and develop what they are playing, and to provide them with additional tools, knowledge and opportunities to further develop themselves. This is usually common amongst a troupe that has been together for some time, and is preparing for a performance.

At this level, the coach would pay less attention to embedding the rules, as the troupe may have

Teaching, coaching and directing have a degree of overlap, yet are different disciplines.

a style of their own that they are cultivating; in preparation the coach should be familiar with this, by making a point of seeing the troupe in action beforehand, so he or she can discuss what they are looking for.

The benefit for the troupe is that a coach will have an impartial eye on what they are doing, and can call out any bad habits they see in any of the players. They can also bring a sense of balance to the group, as sometimes a group can have an alpha figure that can take over every scene. Bringing a balance allows introverted players to get involved, which is important because some people need more space and time. Their offer is just as valid, and they should be allowed space to enter the scene.

Optimal skills for a coach are these:

- To have a proven track record of teaching and performing.
- To have a good sense of self-awareness.
- To have increased self-confidence.
- To gather a good understanding of the individuals being coached: is there a demographic imbalance that may not allow a voice to some people?
- To be open to feedback, and to keep the experience a two-way street.

A good approach for a coach is to act as with less experienced peers, and to remember that they are not expected to have all the answers. Instead, a coach should be pushing the players to ask themselves more questions, as this will improve them as improvisers, and will also enhance the work they are doing. This can be done using open-ended questions that encourage critical thinking, and allow the troupe they are working with to come to their own conclusions. You are coaching the people, not the scene or game.

A coach might proceed in the following manner:

- Avoid questions that give a yes/no answer: keep questions open.
- Avoid 'why' questions because they can put people on the defensive.
- Investigate what other offers are on the table.
- If a different path had been chosen, what could have happened?

Having a conversation where the coach 'unpacks' the scene can help both players and coach learn, as different perspectives are opened up. This can help players be more open-minded next time they are in a scene.

DIRECTING

Directing improvisation takes the previous roles to the next level up. At this point the players would probably have a similar level of experience and capability, and the director's interaction with them would be considered a peer relationship. The director shouldn't need to keep an eye on the best practices of improv as the players would be at a level where all the skills are now second nature. With newer members to the troupe the director might now and then dip back to one of the other leading roles (teacher or coach), and would generally allow the more experienced members to follow their own creative process.

The director's job here is to represent the eye of the audience. However, not all long-running troupes have a designated director, and that can also work, although a sense of hierarchy can help when it comes to driving decisions and making certain production choices.

How the group is directed can differ depending on the type of show they are putting on. If it is a long-form show, then the director would focus on the long-form structure the show would take. For example, if it were to be a Harold, then the director might focus on helping the players be aware of the timings of each act, ensuring that it was evenly balanced and that the actors were creating strong characters for the audience to believe in, and that they drove forwards a storyline for each thread.

If the long-form show had a certain theme, which could be a genre such as horror, murder mystery, space adventure or sitcom (based on audience suggestions), or a musical-based show, then the director would make sure that the players stayed true to the theme.

If the show is short form or a mix of short and long form, then a director would usually be responsible for the selection and casting of the short-form games. For a two-hour run of short-form games, the director would think about the pacing of the games, making sure the energy had an incremental growth as it progressed – including fast-paced games with slow burners. This is again to make sure the audience doesn't get bored, and at the same time overwhelmed by what's happening on stage.

For short-form improv you also have the opportunity to create new formats in the rehearsal space. There are times when this could happen by accident, where in a scene a game may organically occur: if it is spotted and extracted properly, it can be converted into a stand-alone short-form game. In the case of new game creation, the director would again be responsible for finding the funny, acting as the eye of the audience.

Also the director would be responsible for scheduling rehearsal times and providing the rehearsal space, and in essence would be more like a producer in that respect. They could choose to delegate this work out to the other members of the troupe.

BUILDING A TEAM

There is no secret to how you build a successful improv team. As it is an ensemble of the individuals you meet along your learning journey, players tend to connect with certain people they meet in their training, or who in some cases could be mentored by a more senior player or teacher/coach, which in time leads to a formal group. Eventually the group finally settles on a style or theme that they enjoy performing, and this becomes a signature of the troupe. This is important if you want to build a following.

It is not unusual for the members to change over time, with people leaving for whatever reason and new people joining, but with established improv groups the theme, or style, or you might even call it the culture of the group always seems

What not to do when building a team. It is usually better for a troupe to be diverse in gender, race and age, then each person can bring their own individuality to the stage.

to remain the same. This might be considered like a rock band: they might change the musicians' overtime, but if you break it down, Fleetwood Mac is still Fleetwood Mac, Guns n' Roses is still Guns n' Roses, and their following tends to stay loyal. With improv a lot of this has to do with handing down the mantle of the artistic director.

The unfortunate truth of troupe creation is that, as in life in general, we all tend to want to work with people who look and behave as we do – which means we tend to end up seeing groups where everyone is the same. However, this can hold a troupe back, and a good mix of genders, ethnic background, accents and languages is preferable. It can happen that within a country the cast seems to be of a first language (though I can only speak for the improv I have seen in English-speaking countries). When I started out I

LEFT: Action shot from a *Livewired* show.

cool. If the team can keep to an inclusive and diverse ensemble, then it has much more to offer than a team where everyone looks, sounds and reacts the same because they all have a common background, education and upbringing.

Obviously you need and want to have the best talent available to join your group – and remember that an improviser's journey is not over as soon as the training course is finished. People who still have skills to learn and improve on tend to have more drive and ambition than the person who got all the laughs easily – and in time they will surpass their temporarily funnier peers.

PUTTING ON A SHOW

When all is said and done, the real prize is getting out there and presenting your show in front of an audience. We want our friends and family and all those people interested in improv to have a chance to see the magic and beauty of it all. So when the training is done and you have put together a team of improvisers and you are all feeling ready to perform, then do it!

There is no equal for the feeling an improviser gets when their idea is taken on board by their teammates and it flourishes into something magical.

Find a Rehearsal Space

had the same bias, but then I realized that people working in a second language brought with them a different way of thinking, and something special to the group.

Diversity is as important here as it is in any working environment, and for it to work, the team needs to behave in an inclusive manner. Speaking fast, or in a way that certain people cannot understand you, and making that the joke, is not

When looking for a rehearsal space there is no need to be too particular – any space with enough room will do. A private function space in a bar that would not be in use at certain times can come very cheap or even free. Early in the week on an evening when there are no bookings usually works, or even using a space in one of the troupe members' homes. All you need is a chair for each of the cast members and your creativity to practise.

Action shot from a *Livewired* show.

It is good to meet as often as possible, and the more professional your troupe is, then the more often you will want to meet and perfect your craft. At a minimum, meet weekly, regardless of whether you have a show coming up or not, as this builds a bond between the players and also allows people to set their schedule. We all have busy lives, and need a certain structure within the week so we can balance it with our work, partner, children and friends.

Get on social media and promote, promote, promote. Make sure that you reach every and any contact you have.

Assign a Rehearsal Lead

It is important to assign a rehearsal lead, especially if the troupe is run as a democracy without a director or coach. The rehearsal lead should turn up ready with warm-up exercises and a list of items to cover. They could run exercises on any of the above aspects, such as storytelling or character creation or improvised singing. It may depend on what type of show is coming up, and what the team may feel is the current weakness. It can work better if the rehearsal lead stands out of playing for that session and instead focuses on monitoring the scene work and providing feedback for the actors.

Decide on the Style of Show

A show works better if you have a full-time director, but it can also work as a democracy. If you are running a long-form show it is common for three or four troupes to team up and share the evening; the order in which each goes on stage would be worked out in advance.

All shows need an MC to run the night; for long-form shows an MC external to any of the troupes performing would act as a connector between each act. They would open the show, warm up the crowd and introduce each troupe. They would also announce the interval, and would close the show, while promoting the next one, with any classes or community events that might be running close to the time.

After the Show

After the show is a great time to mix with the other improvisers there. If performing is new to your troupe, take some time after the show to socialize and get to know people. This helps build connections and will bring you more performance opportunities. Improvisation nights are a lot of fun, so have some conversations with the audience to get feedback.

It may happen that as an individual you felt you had a poor show, and you might feel disappointed with the evening. This happens to everyone, so don't let it get to you. Improvisation communities are extremely friendly and supportive, so be sure to hang around and get some energy back from people.

If you feel the night could have gone better for you, find a way to help you move on. You might think of the experience as a football match (or any sport or analogy you can think of), and could say to yourself 'I had a bad game, but the team still won and I should enjoy that.'

PRE-PERFORMANCE CHECKLIST

- Make sure you are not hungry/thirsty/tired (have water close by).
- Wear comfortable clothes and shoes so you can move around with ease.
- Arrive at least thirty minutes before the show starts.
- Warm up with your troupe.
- Enter the stage with confidence.
- Be specific with the information you give.
- Make statements (avoid questions).
- Always add: say 'yes' – but if saying 'yes' is not physically possible, then add to the story with your 'no': make sure it is driving something.
- Pay attention to your space work (be consistent).
- Avoid making jokes – play it sincerely.
- If you are a surreal character, make sure there is a grounded character to play against.

9
CORPORATE IMPROV TRAINING

Certain exercises can be converted into training that brings benefit to a corporate environment. Many corporations are now looking to improvisation to help support the development of employees in human skills, and exploring themes such as influencing, collaboration and public speaking, and even to help employees understand more about inclusion and diversity. Improvisation is also used for team building, and is often used as the activity when teams conduct off-site activities or have a global meeting where all the global team may visit one of their offices.

Since the early 2000s improvisation has become increasingly popular with many different types of company, for morale, creativity, and for boosting collaboration. Media and advertising companies use it to help with brainstorming ideas to cultivate advertising and marketing campaigns, as the collaborative nature of improvisation lends itself nicely to group brainstorming and idea sharing, and having these ideas built on. Tech companies use it for all the same reasons, and as a catalyst to bring teams together that might otherwise be siloed – separated from others. This helps partnering teams connect with each other in a fun, interactive way, and instils in them all the positive aspects of improvisation.

Introducing improvisation at a corporate level can be tricky, as you may get people in the room who are not going to take the experience seriously. People with very logical minds may find the activities frivolous and a waste of time, and it can take the facilitator some time to build trust with people who in short do not want to be there.

It is useful to have prepared some things before going into a corporate training session. For example, have a theme for the day: make sure that expectations are set at the very beginning, so the participants have some way of taking back what they learn in the session to their day-to-day jobs.

To open, treat the session as you would a rehearsal or a class in a classroom setting. Start the participants off in a circle where everyone is at an equal standing, and they can all see the facilitator. Setting a safe and friendly space can help people relax.

Opening with a short mindfulness exercise can settle people into the room and calm everyone's nerves. The situation is very different in a corporate training session: unlike in a classroom setting, where people have paid and are committed to attending, here they may have been semi-forced into the training – and as we well know, improvisation is not for everyone. Making everyone comfortable immediately will set a great tone for the rest of the day.

THINKING IN A COLLABORATIVE WAY

Collaboration is a key factor for the success of any company, so introducing fun activities that show how collaboration in improvisation works can really influence the participants in the room. Thinking in a collaborative way is a theme that is easy for them to adhere to, as the basics of the art form of improv are collaborative in nature. In this type of session, you can lean against all the different exercises that instil how we build on each other's ideas in an improvised situation.

Exercise: Dealing with the Frustration of Rejection

To help drive the point home, begin the exercise with the opposite and have people try an exercise where they block or deny any offer from the person they are working with. Instead of leading them straight into a 'Yes! and…' exercise as you might in the classroom, start them off with a 'No' exercise so they can experience in the moment the frustration of rejection. Even though the ask is made up and the rejection has no impact on the participants' lives, the feeling of being blocked is still prevalent in the room. From here, take them to an exercise that forces some kind of negotiation, by replying 'Yes, but…' or 'Maybe that could work!'

This exercise forces the people suggesting to work hard to justify their original point, making collaboration difficult. Then you can lead the participants into a 'Yes, and…' exercise. After it has run for some time, ask people how they felt as they worked through the three exercises. 'Yes, and..' always runs out the favourite.

'What if the suggestion made is stupid?' is often the response from the 'funny' person of the group. To which I would reply:

What we are working on here is cultivating a mindset of collaboration. In the real world people may suggest an idea based on missing data or information that they may not have. If this is the case it is the job of each of us to add that to the conversation in a constructive way. Accepting an idea and giving it the respect and time it deserves allows people to be open and *themselves* when they turn up to work. Making the effort to cultivate this culture makes a stronger team in the long run.

The goal here is to make any idea better, and not to say *my idea* is better.

Exercises to Give Up Control

Other exercises that can help with collaboration are those that force the participants to give up control and allow input from other people, such as one-word story or multi-head, where each player needs to be in the moment and accept the offers that come. It is also a good way for people to see if they force their ideas and opinions aggressively. It is extremely common in improv classes of any kind that when a one-word story game or multi-head game is played, one or more people attempt to give more than one word. This is not done in malice: it is just a person's natural desire to control the narrative.

Convincing people to let this control go and to trust their teammates may take a few attempts, but persevere and it will happen. When a double word is offered against the rules of the game it is another good opportunity to remind the participants that forcing control like this is not allowing the next person to give their input. To have an inclusive work environment you need to allow every person to have a voice and an opportunity to speak.

On the other hand, you don't want the quieter people to hesitate too long and slow the game down. As well as slowing the game and damping down the energy in the room, it also makes the person who hesitates self-conscious and nervous about proceeding. So I follow up with this question to the room:

Have any of you ever been in a situation such as a meeting or work discussion where you've had an idea or something to contribute, and as you thought about it and maybe were about to say something, another person in the meeting does it first? And then the senior person in the room loves the idea?

Inevitably a handful, if not most of the people in the room will admit to having experienced this. But this is a good time to remind them that their instincts are good and that they need to trust them more, and should not be afraid of this failure to deliver. The more you push yourself out there, the easier it gets the next time, and in the same way as going to the gym, it becomes easier the more you go.

Now, play the multi-head game again and remind the people who have been hesitating to trust their instincts, that their contribution is valid, and to be brave. This usually gets everyone to 'up their game' and to go for it. Mistakes are made and recovered, and joy enters the room.

I leave this exercise with this closing thought: 'Be brave and go for it – what's the worst that can happen? You will be right more times than wrong, so when you do get it wrong, nobody will take notice.' This is a great lesson for any corporate team to take away with them.

Fast-Paced Interactive Exercises

Once you have instilled the sense of trusting team-mates and their spontaneity, get them to do some fast-paced interactive exercises, where they have no time to think but must just jump right in. Divide them into teams, depending on the number of people you have in the class. I usually go for three teams of four to five people. Ask each team to give themselves a team name, which they must present to you in a flamboyant manner. To make it interesting and competitive for them you can award points for the most original and flamboyant presentation of a team name.

Next give them a theme, and tell them they will be creating a frozen picture and that points will be awarded for the most creative and original tableau. I generally use the same themes for every class, as this way I can see when an original one happens. For example, ask them to create a picture of a farmyard and give them ten seconds to jump into position. They will scramble around in panic for

a short while, but eventually they will settle on an imitation of some farm animals. What you are looking for here is maybe a group of cows grazing in a field, or a scarecrow surrounded by crows, or a farmer and his wife feeding some chickens – but whatever it is, it needs to be a cohesive picture. If the picture is just random animals scattered around the farm then they are not working together, and it is the cohesive scenario that wins the point.

You can now explain to them what it is you're looking for – a picture where they are all working together – and who has got the point and why. Also explain to them that they are building on the 'Yes, and…' exercise that you have already done. This time they have no time to think – they have to react quickly, look at what someone else has offered, and then jump into position as quickly as possible. Not only is this fast in pace, it is also good fun for them, and brings a lot of joy to the room as it would in any improv training situation.

I then up the complexity to a moving picture (such as a gif) which needs to have one repetitive movement and one repetitive sound, and again award points.

The final version of this exercise is an original play or advert. You can give the players parameters to work round – for example the play needs to have a love story and a long-lost friend, or any parameter you want. If you give them an advert, you can give them the product.

Make sure you remind them to use the 'Yes, and…' and trust spontaneity exercises; allow them several minutes to get it together before performing it in front of the class. This usually brings a nice climax to the day.

Save some time at the end (maybe twenty minutes) to let them use the exercises on a work-related project, or an issue that may be at the forefront of their mind. This way they can apply the exercises directly to a work-related item immediately, and find the value of the exercises. As the facilitator I usually visit each group to make sure no single person is doing all the talking.

ESTABLISHING PRESENCE

Presence is another great aspect from improv to offer to the corporate world, and again there are many exercises that can be used to do this. 9am to 5pm is a long time for an individual to stay focused, and as normal people we can't help but let our minds drift from time to time. In general there is no harm done, and this respite gives our brain a chance to rest while processing information already taken in that day. However, when it begins to interfere with our interaction with other people and processing the information vital to our job, then it can become a cause for worry for some people. And again, this is another expectation and objective for learning I am given by students when they sign up to attend a set of improv classes.

There are neurological conditions that can affect how long and intensely people can stay focused, which we won't discuss here, so we can assume that a person is already aware of how good their focus is, or not.

Presence in a lot of ways can be like meditation. When we meditate, we are training ourselves to keep our thoughts centred, and usually we do this by focusing on our breath; every time our thoughts wander, and we become aware of the wandering, we pull ourselves back to the moment. The more we practise this, the more it becomes second nature.

When we are in a situation where we have to be present, we of course spend our time listening and trying to understand the other person's point of view. However, as we have often experienced, we hear one word or comment, and that triggers our answer and we stop listening and begin to cultivate our response. The danger here is that we stop paying attention to what is being said to us. And getting back into the moment can take a moment.

Exercise: Zip Zap Boing

An exercise that helps people to stay focused is a game called Zip Zap Boing. This game probably has many other names, but was taught to me as Zip Zap Boing (*see* Games Index). Again, bringing a competitive element into the exercise drives the attention span, and when people drop away for whatever reason, they soon come back to the present due to the speed of the exercise.

Another great way to do this is simply to use a ball and have the team keep it in the air for as long as they possibly can; this also drives the need for presence in the moment. If they manage to keep it up twenty times, then see if they can beat it. After a few attempts, ask them what they are doing right now: the answers you are looking for are:

- focusing
- being in the moment
- chasing a single goal
- working together as a team
- sharing success and failure together
- pushing all other thoughts away – this is where we want to be when we are completely present

Exercise: Thinking on Your Feet

For this exercise I use the lines from a hat game, or as it is otherwise known, fishbowl. In this corporate version I give them the 'who, what, where' in advance so the conversation already has some structure. Then I may give them some tips, such as avoid too many questions, and try not to get straight into conflict. When they get their cue, they read the paper and justify it within the context of the conversation they are having. Give them a couple of goes each.

At the end of the session, have each person give a short speech about themselves, and at some point, cue them for a paper that they need to justify. This gives them the opportunity to try the exercise on something they are an expert on: themselves!

EVERYDAY LIFE

For a corporation to be successful it needs people to be happy. A happy person has a varied life filled with experiences that enlighten and stimulate them. Businessmen know this, and offer their workers opportunities to engage with as much of the world as they can. It is not unusual for businesses to have facilities for workers to shower after they cycle/run/walk to work. Also a lot of companies give access to gym membership, and include more spiritual things, such as yoga and meditation.

All these things bring something of value to the individual: mental and physical wellbeing, education, relaxation or fun. Improvisation should be serving a similar purpose. A one-off training is a very short-term win, and for it to become a culture it needs to be conducted on a more regular basis.

A yoga class can help an employee's flexibility and posture, which could be adversely affected by sitting at a desk all day, or a swim at lunchtime helps increase the blood flow and lifts the mood. An improvisation class can help the shy or less extrovert person seize an opportunity by taking charge of the moment, and for the individual who feels they become easily distracted, it could help them stay focused and in the room. However, the facilitator must show *how* it does this by linking it back to a solid day-to-day example or a personal story.

Ultimately corporate training is really taking transferable skills and making them applicable to how people live in the real world.

10
INDEX OF GAMES

This index gives instructions on how to play the following popular games. Each can be treated like an exercise that addresses certain skills already mentioned in the foregoing chapters.

JUST QUESTIONS

Also known as Questions Only, this is a game in which the actors can only converse in questions.

Improvisers face each other and begin by asking the opening questions.

The players must avoid asking a question that does not relate to the situation the characters are in. So it works better if the question relates to what has been asked, not necessarily answering it, but at least addressing it.

To Play

Two players take the stage, and someone is needed to MC the game. The MC will give the players a topic, such as 'You are a couple in the bathroom: go!' The players will start by only asking each other questions. The following is an example of what to avoid:

Player 1: 'Have you seen my watch?'
Player 2: 'Have you seen the frying pan?'

No doubt this answer would get a laugh, but it does not help the scene and so Player 2 should get buzzed out. The following example shows how it could work better:
Player 1: 'Have you seen my watch?'

Player 2: 'Have you looked in your sports bag?'
Player 1: 'Did you borrow my bag when you went to the gym?'
Player 2: 'Yes!' (But this is a statement, so player 2 gets buzzed out.)

The MC should watch for the following:

- The players should address the questions asked, and move the scene forwards.
- Don't let the players hesitate as this means they are overthinking it and getting stuck in their head.
- Get the players to have fun: put them under pressure so they fail.

The point of the exercise is to keep the conversation alive as long as possible, and to have fun. Be spontaneous and don't overthink it.

REVOLVE

This exercise requires four players, who should stand in twos.

All improvisers start in a two-by-two formation, and the first pair are given an ask from the audience on which to improvise.

When the MC signals (usually by desk bell), the group rotates by one person.

To Play

Each pair has a different scene, which means that each actor is in two separate scenes. Usually the MC will call the rotation by ringing a bell on a cliff-hanger. The game generally contains three to four acts in each scene. To begin with give each couple of improvisers a topic with which to open their scene.

The MC should watch for the following:

- It is recommended, but not a rule, that the player entering the scene makes the first offer.
- Encourage the players to find a pattern as they progress to the next scene: this is where the game could be.

- It is recommended, but not a rule, that the story jumps forwards in time.

This is a great exercise for storytelling, and helping the players to find a plot or a pattern.

All improvisers should move together so they don't bump each other.

ABOVE: When in place the new pair are given a different ask from the audience, completely unrelated to the previous one.

On a signal the group rotates again.

Again, the new pair are given an ask from the audience.

The final pair are given an ask, and the scene can begin. The rotation usually happens on a cliff-hanger, when the next scene begins.

MULTI-HEAD

Multi-head is another very popular show game, and great for keeping people in the moment.

To Play

A minimum of seven people is needed for this game; the MC can play the seventh person, who would be the interviewer. Divide the six players into two groups of three people, and have them stand shoulder to shoulder. The illusion of the game is that the group of three are not three people, but one person, and they can only speak one word at a time.

The MC can move the conversation between the two groups, and run it like a television or radio interview. It can also be run off other platforms, such as a therapy session or a political debate.

The improvisers are lined up. Linking arms is optional, depending on how comfortable they are. Linking arms gives the impression that they are representing one person.

The MC should watch for the following:

- If the group of three make an illogical statement, it is fun to dive into this.
- Keep the conversation on track as much as possible, and keep a good balance between both multi-heads.

• If doing this as part of a show, end on a high.

This is a fun game for breaking the ice in a class or rehearsal.

The players are interviewed by the MC, and speak one word in turn.

The transition between improvisers may be slow to start with, so encourage them to pick up the pace.

The improvisers usually decide when they have reached the end of a sentence, by pausing.

STORY DIE

Story Die is very popular as part of a short-form show; it is also a great warm-up exercise.

To Play

The MC will ask the team to stand in a line, in a shallow arc so they can hear each other. They must ask for a hero and a trip or quest. Players can only speak if they are being pointed at by the MC; when the MC points to another player, this one must take over the sentence.

The MC should watch for the following:

- Players must not hesitate – if they do, they are out of the game.
- Players must take over the sentence seamlessly, and even take over mid-word.
- They must avoid the same word, but focusing on thoughts of the hero, they can move the story forwards with actions.
- Be ruthless, so they are knocked out quickly: make it fun to fail.
- Get advanced players to do a round in a chosen accent, or give them other challenges, such as speaking in rhyme or Shakespearean verse.

The improvisers line up facing out towards the audience.

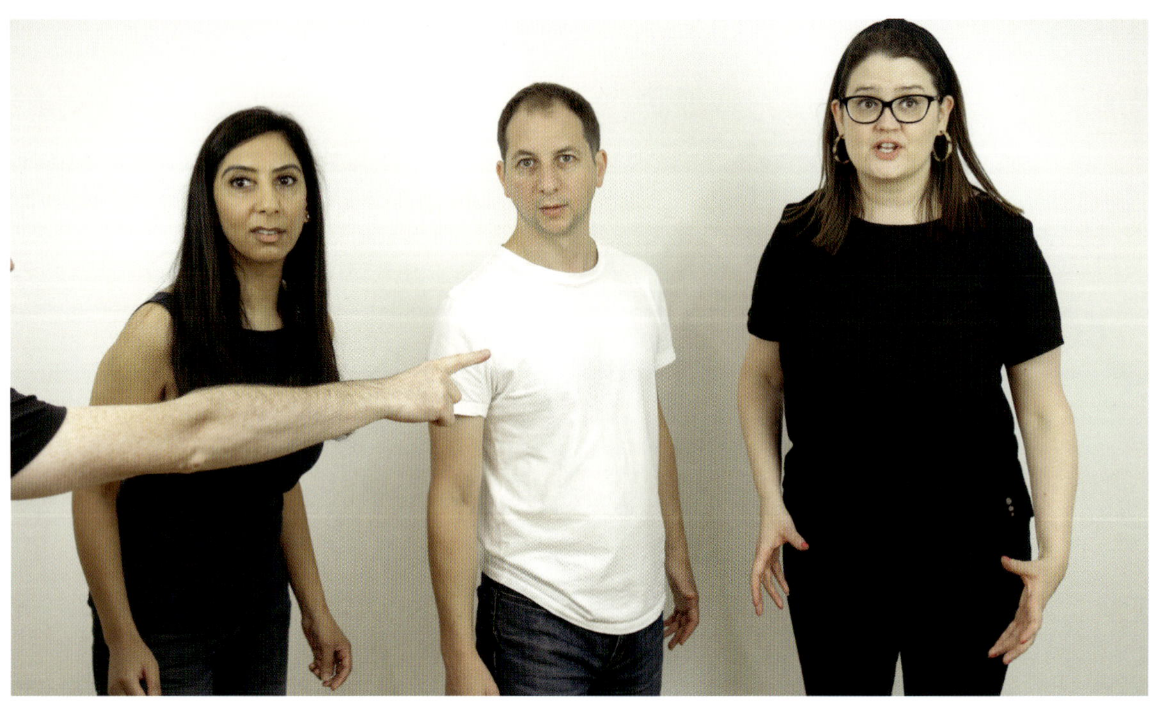

The MC points at one improviser, and the player gives their input to the story. When the MC moves his arm the speaking improviser stops, and the next improviser he points to must continue.

When an improviser makes a mistake, they are sent off by the other players; the game ends when only one improviser is left.

ONE-WORD STORY

Players should stand in a circle, and will tell a story, where each person adds to the story one word at a time.

To Play

The game begins by asking for a character, and a trip or aspiration for the hero. The MC should let the circle know in which direction the story will be going. The MC can start with a word.

The MC should watch for the following:

- People should not wait too long to contribute their word.
- If people are asking for the last word to be repeated, players should be asked to speak more clearly and loudly.

- People should avoid forcing verbs or nouns into the story where it breaks the grammar of the story.
- If this happens, remind players that any contribution is necessary, even if it is just a filler word such as 'a', 'or', 'the': these words must be there for the story to make sense, so don't think you are being left out if that's what you add.

FOREIGN FILM

This game requires four people: two actors and two translators.

To Play

The actors are given a foreign language that they will pretend to speak, and an enigmatic name of an art house-type film. The actors begin acting in the

The stage setting is with the actors up centre stage, while the translators are positioned downstage left and right.

The actors speak and their translator follows.

foreign language. The translators, who are off stage, will then translate the dialogue for the audience. It is important that the dialogue moves in a rotated fashion: Actor 1 – Translator 1\ Actor 2 – Translator 2: this gives the players some structure and removes any confusion about who speaks next.

The MC should watch for the following:

• Make sure the dialogue keeps its structure so the players and audience are always clear on who is translating for who.

• Encourage the actors on stage to introduce objects and high emotions; it is up to the translators to then sort it out.

• The translators can also make big offers to the actors and make them do things. The fun in this game is the collaboration between the actor\ translator in making a character understood, and also getting each other into trouble.

The flow should go actor 1 –> translator 1 –> actor 2 –> translator 2.

UNSUITABLE APPLICANT

Unsuitable Applicant is a guessing game and requires four players.

To Play

The first player is the interviewer, who is looking to hire a new employee for their business. The other three players are applying for the job.

Before the interviewer leaves the room, the audience will decide what kind of business they run or own, and what kind of employee they need to hire (what position they are hoping to fill). When the applicants are not there, decide with the audience or class which of the three is unsuitable for the role they are applying for. For example, if they are applying for a position as a librarian, they

The improvisers playing the applicants are set upstage left, while the interviewer stands at stage right.

The interviewer calls each in turn to ask questions and get clues.

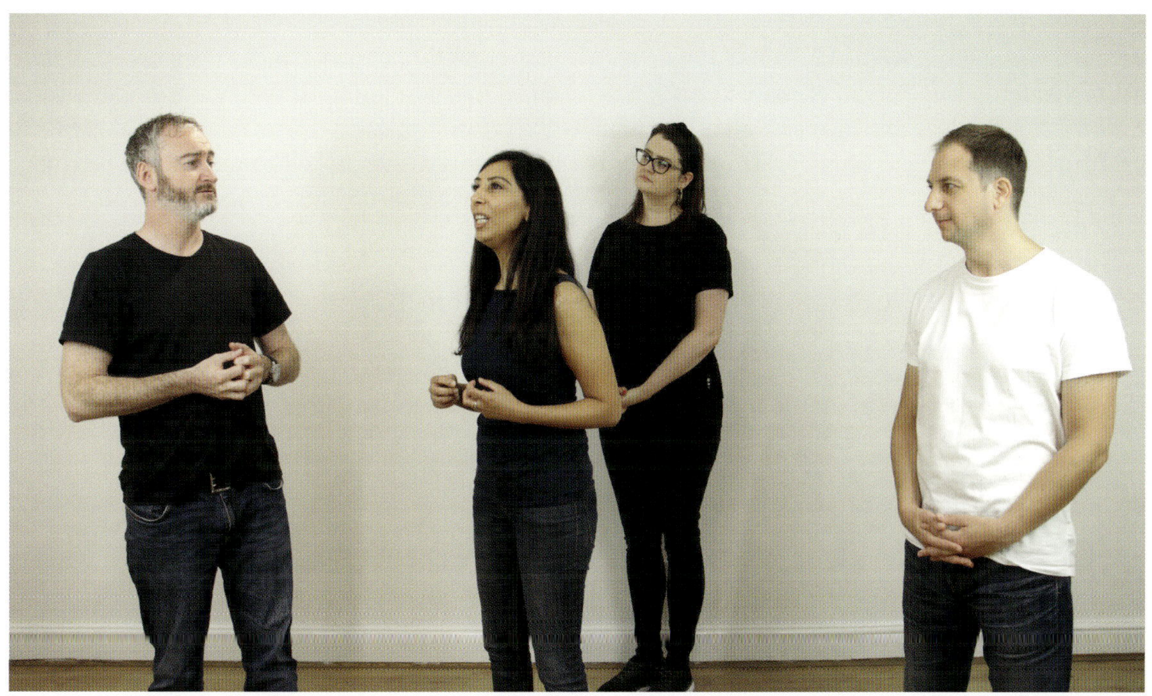

Each applicant will give information incrementally on their character.

The interviewer maintains control of the stage by calling each improviser if they need to get more clues to figure out their character.

will be unsuitable if they prefer films to books and always watch a film instead of reading books, or if they are very social and love to chat all the time with customers.

Try and avoid giving people disabilities, even invisible ones such as dyslexia or colour blindness, as this can make the people watching uncomfortable.

Best practice for this game is to ask the same three questions to each applicant, and for them to give a demonstration at the end. Each answer can give a bit more away about their unsuitability.

The MC should watch for the following:

- Encourage the applicants to give their clues as to their unsuitability incrementally: try not to give all away too soon.
- The MC – as the interviewer – should mix around the questions to avoid the same person going first each time.
- The interviewer oversees the game once it starts, so make sure the applicants only speak when addressed by the interviewer.
- The fun here is for the applicants to play with the audience by giving subtle clues at first, and then making it more obvious. The interviewer can also play with the applicants if they have figured out their unsuitability early.

SEANCHAÍ

Seanchaí is an Irish term referring to a storyteller who tells the story in the third person, so the storyteller is not the protagonist nor a character in the story.

To Play

The logistics of the story is that the narrator or seanchaí begins the story, and after the introduction there is a swap between the players and the storyteller. They must be careful not to repeat what has just been said or acted: instead they confirm it, and then move the story to another offer. This is good for the concept of storytelling and using 'Yes, and…'. This game is also played in similar forms called The Narrator or The Novelist.

The MC should watch for the following:

- Make sure that when the story moves from the narrator to the actors, or vice versa, they don't simply repeat what was just said.
- If this is happening, then make sure the narrator gives more open-ended offers to the actors; the last line should therefore be non-descriptive.

FREEZE TAG

Freeze Tag is an old, well-known game that is better suited to rehearsal then shows.

To Play

Two players are given a separate activity and told to freeze. They then start the scene; their task is to justify why they are in that position, and at the same time establish the 'who, what, where'. The scene ends with one of the players off stage shouting 'Freeze!' and tagging one of the players out and taking their place, in exactly the same position. The entering player then needs to start the next scene, preferably by initiating a 'who, what, where'.

The MC should watch for the following:

- A common cheat in this exercise is for one of the players to make it a coaching scene: they will open by telling the other actor that whatever it is they are doing, it is wrong, and they need to copy them.
- Make sure that the person calling 'Freeze!' and entering takes up the same position as the person they are tagging out.
- Encourage the off-stage players to be brave and call out 'Freeze!'; the scenes should be no more than thirty seconds each.

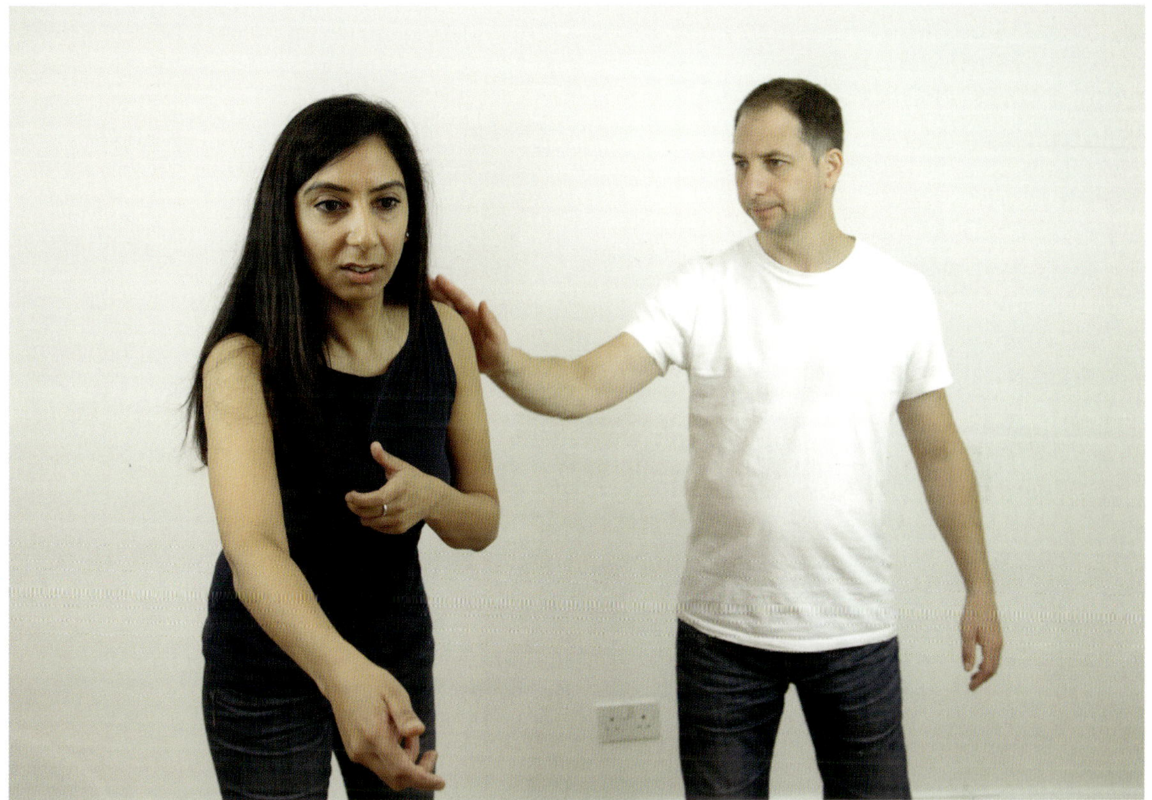

An improviser is entering to tag another out and take their place in a new scene.

• There is also a blind version of this game, where the next player to enter is facing away and cannot see the action on stage; this means that they have less time to make a choice and need to be more spontaneous.

LINES FROM A HAT (ALSO KNOWN AS FISHBOWL)

At some point each member of the cast, or students, or audience should write some lines on pieces of paper. These lines should be short questions or statements, they should not contain proper names, and the handwriting must be clear. It is also helpful to avoid topical subjects, as these tend to take over.

To Play

The game is usually played with two players, who are given a situation in which to act. They will set up a 'who, what, where', and once the scene is settled, the MC will ring a bell or give a signal to the players to take a piece of paper from the hat or fishbowl.

Different improv companies play this in various ways, but it is more fun and beneficial if the person who reads the sentence is the one to justify it. The other player should avoid helping them unless it is necessary.

The MC should watch for the following:

• The players must give each other enough space to justify their paper.

The scene starts with the usual 'who, what, where'.

When the scene is established, one improviser will be given a line from the hat; if it is not their turn to speak when they receive it, they hide it until it is their turn.

When the time is right, the improviser reads the line out loud. The first time they see the line is as they read it.

- The sentence must be justified sufficiently before moving on with the scene.
- Remind the player that the more normal they keep the scene, the better it is, as they will have random input coming from the papers.

MEANWHILE

Meanwhile is a great game/exercise for warming up before a show. It is usually started off with a single word, and the scene can be short. The MC may call something like 'meanwhile at the farmyard', and the player then rushes in and begins this scene.

This is a great opportunity to play animals or inanimate objects. The scene could be about farmyard animals discussing a day in their lives, or farm tools or machinery doing the same.

Meanwhile is a great exercise for spontaneity and space work.

REFERENCES AND BIBLIOGRAPHY

Books

Halpern, C. (2006). *Art by Committee*. Meriweather Publishing

Halpern, C. (1994). Close, D. & Johnson, K. *Truth in Comedy*. Meriweather Publishing

Johnstone, K. (1987). *Impro*. Bloomsbury Academic

Joseph Campbell Foundation (2008). *The Hero with a Thousand Faces*. New World Library

Knight, R. (2018) *Mime the Gap*. The Crowood Press

Salinsky, T. & Frances-White, D. (2008) *The Improv Handbook*. Bloomsbury

Spolin, V. (1999) *Improvisation for the Theatre* (3rd ed.) Northwestern University Press

Theatre/plays

Carthaginians – Frank McGuiness, 1988

Our Town – Thornton Wilder, 1938

Romeo and Juliet – William Shakespeare, c.1592–95

Stones in His Pockets – Marie Jones, 1996

Film and TV

Arrested Development, created by Mitchell Hurwitz. Fox Broadcasting Company, 2003–2006

Family Guy, created by Seth MacFarlane. Fox Broadcasting Company, 1999–present

Fantastic Beasts and Where To Find Them, directed by David Yates, produced by David Heyman, J. K. Rowling, Steve Kloves & Lionel Wigram, 2016

Fawlty Towers, created by John Cleese & Connie Booth. BBC, 1975–1979

Goodfellas, directed by Martin Scorsese, produced by Irwin Wrinkler, 1990

Inception, directed by Christopher Nolan, produced by Christopher Nolan and Emma Thomas, 2010

Jaws, directed by Steven Spielberg, produced by Richard D. Zanuck and David Brown, 1975

Moneyball, directed by Bennet Miller, produced by Michael De Luca, Rachael Horovitz & Brad Pitt, 2011

Oceans 11, directed by Steven Soderberg, produced by Jerry Weintraub, 2001

Rocky, directed by John G. Avildsen, produced by Irwin Winkler & Robert Chartoff, 1976

The Sopranos, created by David Chase, HBO, 1999–2007

Star Wars, directed by George Lucas, produced by Lucasfilm, 1977

The Two Ronnies – 'Four Candles' sketch, written by Ronnie Barker. BBC, 1976

Warrior, directed by Gavin O'Connor, produced by Gavin O'Connor, Greg O'Connor, David Mimran & Jordan Schur, 2009

Websites

https://spolingamesonline.org

www.groundlings.com/

www.livewiredimprov.com

www.secondcity.com/

www.theannoyance.com/

www.uprightcitizens.org/

www.violaspolin.org

Armstrong, P. (2010). 'Bloom's Taxonomy'. Vanderbilt University Center for Teaching. https://cft.vanderbilt.edu/guides-sub-pages/blooms-taxonomy/

McLeod, S. A. (2020). 'Maslow's hierarchy of needs'. Simply Psychology. https://www.simplypsychology.org/maslow.html

INDEX